Sushi and Fries

How cultural differences hinder Japanese companies
from succeeding in Europe

Des Collins

Published by New Generation Publishing in 2014

First Edition

www.newgeneration-publishing.com

New Generation Publishing

To my wife Susan for putting up with me and my ideas.

Introduction

At 3 o'clock on a Tuesday afternoon in January 2012, an email arrived in my inbox from the manager of the Human Resources department. It was directed to an executive in an outplacement consultancy. Because it was written in Dutch, a language I do not speak, I suspected that it had been copied to me by mistake. As it was only three lines long, I read it over several times and slowly began to understand the content. It announced the company's decision to dismiss one of its vice presidents the following week. It described the person as having an English mother tongue and having more than thirty years' service with the company. There was only one person in the company that fit the description – me!

Two short hours later, the newly appointed chief executive officer of Bridgestone was informing me that he wanted to create a new team and that I would not be a part of it. He assured me that there was nothing personal in the decision and that it was not a reflection on my performance. Yet, it was difficult to be reassured about the former when I learned that the management team had decided to end my contract on January 23rd - one day before the annual New Year's reception at which the loyalty of long-serving employees would be celebrated. There was only one person in the company who had passed the thirty year mark in the preceding twelve months – me!

Soon after the meeting, I was out in the cold and wet January evening armed only with a few personal belongings and thirty years of memories. I had given the best part of my adult professional life to my Japanese employer; I had travelled the world, negotiated successfully with some very big corporations, and I had experienced business at a level I had never dreamed of in my youth. However, I also witnessed the culture shock experienced by employees as they attempted to integrate with their Japanese employer, or even just understand what was expected of them. Many employees failed to adapt and meet the expectations of their boss so they were forced to leave the company. I saw a situation where staff turnover was chronically high and where business development was blocked and creativity choked by bad management. Over and over, I saw new managers posted to Europe from Japan who thought that they could change the company and make it more Japanese.

The reader might well ask why I stayed in the company for such a long time. My father used to say that I was caught in a fur-lined trap. He thought that the remuneration and benefits that I enjoyed were preventing me from escaping to a career where I might feel more fulfilled. While there might be some truth in that opinion, it was also true that I have always been fascinated by communication between cultures, and how easily we misunderstand each other. As well, I derived great satisfaction from working with distinct cultures whose diversity provided both an opportunity to develop an empathetic and flexible dialogue with business leaders whose contexts were very different from my own, and an intellectual challenge that I was forced to resolve over and over again.

My experiences working with a Japanese international company were extensive, and I can confidently assert that I learned something new every day. In the process, I accumulated a great deal of insight into the complex relationships between Japanese and European business and cultures and concluded that what I had learned could be of great benefit to others. I spent sixteen years in the European headquarters of Bridgestone. During that time, the CEO and other top positions were filled by Japanese men on short overseas assignments. As a vice president I was among the highest positioned Europeans in the company and I had to try and bridge the gap between the boardroom and the European employees. My job necessitated regular travel to Japan and daily interaction with Japanese colleagues both in Japan and in Europe. As a native English speaker, I was used as a speech writer for the highest level of the Board, and this required my good understanding of what the CEO messages and policy were. At the same time I managed a team of Europeans of different nationalities, and had to help them with their cross cultural difficulties.

My career progression from a telephone salesman in my home country, Ireland, to vice president of the European organisation with a turnover in excess of 3 billion Euros, was unusual and filled with extraordinary moments. As I moved forward, I realised that the communication problems that exist between cultures have a huge impact on the ability of an organisation to succeed, and that these very important challenges are often not recognised by those who lead those organisations.

In the early 1980s, I started working in telesales for ECI, a company that held a sole distribution agreement for Bridgestone tyres in Ireland. At that time, it seemed that Japanese industry was on a path to take over the world. We were surrounded by fast growing Japanese brands; Toyota, Nissan, Honda, Yamaha, Mitsubishi, Sony, Pioneer, Pentax, Olympus, Nikon. These as well as many other corporations were bringing quality new products to the market and were rapidly changing people's perception of Japanese goods and Japan itself. When a representative from the Bridgestone Corporation made a rare visit to Ireland, it was akin to having the president of the United States come to visit. We were awed by these people who had travelled half way around the world to see us. In those days, many Japanese companies were developing their European sales networks through trading houses and sole distributor agreements. The Japanese companies benefitted from their distributor's knowledge of the local market, and in return invariably granted generous profit margins to the distributors. Over the next thirty years, this situation evolved gradually to become owned distribution where the Japanese corporation, whether Toyota or Bridgestone, owned and managed its own distribution channels in each country. This led to the corporations imposing their own operating models on the distribution chain including "how to sell" and "one size fits all" promotion methods.

In 1989, Bridgestone decided to set up its own distribution company in Ireland. I was invited to become its first general manager. After two successful years in the position, I was appointed managing director. The success of the Irish subsidiary had been recognised with awards for Best European Sales Company, and the Bridgestone brand was firmly established in the Irish automotive industry.

In 1997, I was invited to join the European headquarters based in Brussels. I left Ireland and took the opportunity to advance my career in Belgium. The biggest immediate challenges were all related to cultural differences and the communication issues that derived from them. Having come from a subsidiary where contact with Japanese executives was limited to meetings with them 3 or 4 times a year when I reported to headquarters or at board meetings, I was now working with Japanese colleagues above and below me on a daily basis. So began my mountain climb.

I negotiated the obstacles carefully, rising through director positions and on to my appointment as vice president in 2001. As Vice President of Sales & Marketing, I was responsible for the subsidiary sales companies across Europe as well as two remaining sole distributors in Norway and Greece. All business situations had to be handled on two levels. The first was to solve problems and develop the business within company strategies. The second was to prepare and present business cases to the Japanese management in a way that they could understand them. Consequently, ostensibly easy decisions could take a very long time, and, as some of the stories included in this book will show, could lead to lost opportunities.

After five years in sales and marketing, I transferred to the public relations department as its vice president, a role that evolved over the following years to include corporate brand development and European government relations. My final job was as Vice President, European Communications. The wide variety of roles that I performed in the company gave me direct contact with many Japanese managers and employees all over the world.

I developed a deep respect for Japanese culture. I admired the integration of many Japanese individuals into varying European contexts: they made friends, learned European languages, travelled all over Europe and added value to the company for which they worked. But I also realised that there were many others who came to Europe with preconceived ideas and prejudices about the countries to which they had been posted and with a closed mind and little consideration for the opinions of local staff with whom they would collaborate.

In preparing to write this book, I discovered that many books have been written to explain how westerners should behave when dealing with Japanese businesses or visiting Japan as tourists. While I have referred to some of these, my intention was to write from a very different perspective and for a very different purpose. To begin with, Amelie Nothomb's *Fear and Trembling* and Niall Murtagh's *The Blue-eyed Salaryman* deal with the difficulties of working as the only European in a Japanese company in Japan. In both cases, they had chosen to step inside a Japanese company in its home base. In my book, it is the overseas subsidiary of a Japanese company that employees join and this is where the clash of cultures comes to the surface: I wanted to examine the consequences of the profound cultural differences between the East and the West through the prism of my experience working for a Japanese company in Europe.

I use real-life stories taken from my experience and I explore the cultural differences that lead to conflict and misunderstandings between Japanese and Europeans. I use the true stories to illustrate the difficulties faced by any European working in a Japanese work environment as well as the obstacles that Japanese managers face in Europe. By taking this approach, there was a risk that some of the stories, which are all true, could be considered as a betrayal of confidentiality so I have changed the names of all those involved and made every effort to avoid disclosing confidential information.

My hope is that my experience will help European managers who work in Japanese companies and who are concerned about their own lack of progress in Europe to identify some of the key obstacles on the path up the mountain. The true stories that I tell may help them to realise that they are not alone. I also hope that they will find some of the responses I believe can help to overcome their difficulties. The stories in this book are also important for anyone who is considering working for a Japanese specifically or Asian company more generally and who is struggling to understand the pervasive business culture. Finally, I am anticipating that Japanese managers may learn something about classic "errors" that they should avoid when working in Europe if they aspire to greater success.

Chapter 1

Japanese Management in Action

I consider myself to be open-minded with a willingness to accept and understand different behaviours and cultures. While I have worked closely with some difficult, arrogant and rude individuals in my long career with a Japanese company, I have also made and kept good friends with many Japanese colleagues. Over the years, I have learned an important lesson: do not generalise when describing "the Japanese". It would be wrong to give the impression that there is a management style that is specifically Japanese or that there is a method that is the monopoly of the Japanese. Nevertheless, I will share some of my experiences because I believe they highlight some of the on-going challenges that Japanese companies fail to resolve when working in non-Japanese contexts.

Let me begin by describing a particularly unpleasant experience I had as a vice-president of sales, reporting directly to a Japanese manager.

Handling People

Joe, an American, was managing director of a respected company in the United Kingdom; he was in his early fifties and he had had a long and successful career with Firestone Corporation. But Firestone had been taken over by the Japanese tyre giant Bridgestone Corporation. On this day, Joe is standing in front of a room of 30 people; his shoulders are sagging, his face is red and his eyes are wet.

In the front row of the room, a famous Japanese executive, Unaji is sitting down. He is short, squat, and overweight. He has no visible neck to support his oversized face which can change expression without warning. Anyone who had ever had the misfortune of working with Unaji remembered him. He was renowned, even amongst Japanese employees, for his treatment, or mistreatment, of staff, colleagues and especially of his direct reports.

Unaji was not only famous for his rudeness; he was also legendary for setting unrealistic targets. Every half year, he set a budget with growth rates that could never be achieved, and consequently de-motivated sales staff who knew they could never attain their bonus levels. For almost four years he ran his division in military fashion, instilling fear in everyone who worked with him. While he never actually fired anyone, many who refused to work in such an atmosphere, left the company. He dismissed the leavers as "weak".

And yet, he could be jovial and charming when he wanted to be. First impressions of those who met him socially were generally that he was one of the most pleasant people they had ever met.

But on this day, Unaji was at his bulldog best.

"How dare you come here and present figures like this" roared Unaji and, pointing his finger aggressively at Joe, demanded, "Do you want to resign your position?" The room was filled with staff from headquarters who were obliged to listen to the presentation of the sales and financial budget for the coming year. Many of those in the room were junior trainees, but there were also a number of middle and higher managers present. As the castigation continued, a close colleague whispered to me, "I feel physically sick". I knew what he meant. I was in shock and certain that somewhere there had to be laws forbidding such intimidating behaviour.

Every time Joe tried to open his mouth to give an explanation, Unaji shouted him down. No explanation or reasoning would be heard." You should be ashamed of yourself," barked Unaji.

My discomfort was worsened by the knowledge that the budget Joe was presenting had been prepared at a time when the strong value of the British pound was causing many UK businesses to suffer from what is called *parallel imports*, where the same products from weaker currency markets are imported at lower prices instead of through the official channels. In other words, there was a perfectly valid reason to explain why the UK budget could not match the growth demanded by headquarters.

On this particular day, as Unaji repeatedly interrupted and screamed at Joe, I had a troubling thought. I actually began to wonder whether Unaji was, in fact, laying down markers for the rest of the team about complying with his wishes and targets, or if he was deriving sadistic pleasure from what he was doing so publicly to Joe.

After the incident, what became clear was that Joe was a changed man. He had been stripped of his self-confidence, and found himself caught in an apparently irreconcilable struggle between what he believed was right for the company and what Unaji demanded of him. His long service with the company ended soon afterwards.

Unpredictability

Unaji's unpredictability was probably the most difficult aspect for employees at Bridgestone to deal with. At times, he could surprise us with insights or understandings that were as timely as they were enlightening; at other times, his bullying rages would erupt for no apparent reason. One just never knew what to expect from Unaji.

One day, a teleconference was arranged with our Finnish company, and I was quite sure that it was going to be ugly. The managing director of the Finnish company, Mikka, was often a target for Unaji's outbursts. Before the meeting, I sought out Unaji to tell him that Mikka's father was critically ill in hospital and that Mikka had spent most of the night at his bedside. Unaji roared, "Are you asking me to go easy on him? Is this some kind of excuse?" I replied that I thought it would be better if he understood the situation before the meeting, and that he could do as he pleased. He was annoyed that I had told him.

Yet, when some months later, just before another teleconference with Mikka, I informed Unaji that Mikka's dog had died the previous night, he reacted with extraordinary compassion. "Is Mikka OK?" he asked. "The loss of a dog can have a terrible effect on a person," he told me, and suggested that, "Maybe we should cancel the teleconference." I understood that the mood of the day determined his reactions; that the nature or the gravity of the loss a person incurred was irrelevant to him. Nothing was predictable.

The Revolving Door

After four years in Europe, Unaji was repatriated to Japan. The relief amongst those who survived his tenure was palpable. A new Japanese incumbent was announced. No-one in Europe knew him and we all waited nervously not knowing what to expect. Shinagawa appeared small and gentle, even frail, but he exuded confidence and authority. When he spoke, people listened. He was a no-nonsense executive. Although he shook up teams and replaced weaker performers, he somehow avoided unnecessary disruption and stress. He was the first Japanese boss that I could approach and talk to. He made time to listen and to discuss. He would challenge a hypothesis, seek different opinions on business issues, and consider various options before making decisions. However, once made, his decision was non-negotiable. Even if his team did not always fully agree with his choice, they implemented it because it was generally agreed that he consulted widely, treated those with whom he worked fairly, and that he respected the ideas of European managers. As a result, Shinagawa was highly regarded.

While he remained a tough task master with high expectations, people were happy to work harder and longer because he shared his vision and because he provided opportunities for those who worked with him to propose and implement important business projects. Unsurprisingly, the company results improved greatly during the period Shinagawa was CEO. His approach to managing a European organisation was a lesson to all foreign companies. However, in spite of his success, Bridgestone replaced him after less than three years in charge. This was a critical error because the European company was negatively affected by his departure.

In the case of someone of the calibre of Shinagawa, it was comprehensible that he should be called to global headquarters where, a few years later, he was appointed global CEO and president. Unlike other CEOs, Shinagawa was very effective during his short tenure and restructured the company for future success.

The key to his strategy was to build a mid-term plan. He began with an analysis of the market demand and an assessment of the realistic growth potential of the company. Then, because the necessary supply chain and manufacturing capacity was identified, the investments that were required became clear. Then calculation of the operating expenses alongside these plans indicated the forecasted profit and return on assets. The preparation of this plan took several months of analysis and preparation by each department in the company, but the result was a realistic plan that justified the necessary investment. It would be difficult to argue that this was not a best practice approach that would be valid for any company.

This seemingly straight-forward methodology had hitherto been missing in the European company, and if management in Europe continued to change its CEOs as regularly as it did, it was very unlikely that it was going to be possible to make this coherent kind of leadership practice a commonplace reality.

To do or not to do?

Japanese culture demands that individuals follow a code of behaviour in almost every social setting. Many of the codes have their roots in ancient times and have survived the test of time.

During a two week training course in Tokyo, a Japanese coach introduced me to some of these codes. The first lesson initiated me into the art of the bow. Greeting with a bow has its ancient roots in Samurai history and simulates the codes of warrior behaviour. Like the handshake, the bow can convey a salutation, a farewell, or an expression of thanks and gratitude.[1]

When two Japanese are introduced to each other, they bow. The depth of the bow is indicative of the social or business status of each. If person A is a high ranking person, then person B will bow very low. If person A knows that person B is not from as high a status as himself, then he will bow, but not as low as person B is bowing. If two Japanese are introduced to each other and neither knows which of them has the higher status then they will both bow low, sometimes taking it in turn and repeating the process as if to say, "You are more important than I am". This can continue for three or four bows each, even as both look out of the corner of their eyes to note how low the other is bowing so they can measure how low their next bow must be. I have seen cases where two men have banged their heads together because they were unable to see each other anymore.

Some years later, armed with my knowledge of the intricacies of the

---

[1] F.Darren Smith, *To Bow or not to Bow* 2003
http://www.shitoryu.org/heritage/bowing.htm

bow, I prepared to greet the corporation's president on his visit to Europe. As he stepped into the room surrounded by his entourage and as he approached me, I stepped into open space and bowed as low as I could. I was greeted with loud laughter. I was embarrassed but even more than that, I was puzzled. When I asked Japanese colleagues what I had done wrong, they assured me that I had done nothing wrong but informed me that such behaviour was not expected from westerners, especially when outside Japan. It seemed that even though I had been coached on how to bow, I still had not learned when to do so.

I have since learned that when greeting a Japanese person in Europe the safest thing to do is to bow about 20 degrees - with eyes down of course. If greeting a Japanese person in Japan, then it is better to bow from the waist to about 40 degrees but only for about two seconds.

Another custom which is codified and which is surprisingly complex to understand is the order in which people stand in a lift. In Japan, the most senior person, or the one with the highest status, will stand at the back of the lift, in the corner furthest from the operating buttons. The most junior person, or if there is a mix of sexes in the lift, the most junior female, will normally stand at the front of the lift and will assume the role of lift operator. At each floor stop, he or she will exit the lift, eyes down, and stand back to allow the more senior people to exit or enter the lift, before resuming his or her place.

To watch this process in real time is fascinating. Everyone finds their correct position effortlessly. Body language is used subtly but very effectively: the senior person exudes authority and status; the junior person exudes deference. The junior person is in some ways the most interesting: it is almost as if he or she is apologising for being in the same lift. Eyes are down; the body is perfectly still. The only sound is the unspoken longing of the subordinate to exit the lift at the earliest opportunity.

For Europeans in the lift, it is almost impossible to discern the status of the group so standing towards the front of the lift turns out to be a safe bet. Even then, junior people feel uncomfortable if they are forced to stand behind a westerner especially if the westerner is older. Over time, I learned that the natural position for the older people is at the back and the youngest in the front.

Once again, this custom has its roots in warrior behaviour. The place farthest from the door is the safest place whether standing in a lift or in a room. Enemies enter and attack through doors.

But the codes extend even further and lay other traps for Europeans. Generally, Europeans prefer to sit in the front passenger seat of a car. Japanese protocol is that the most important passenger sits behind the driver, and the lowest ranking person sits in the front passenger seat. The rationale for this is that the place behind the driver is the safest, and that the front passenger seat is the most dangerous.

This preoccupation with positions continues at the dining table. The place of honour is in the middle of the side farthest from the door and with a view on the door. This allows the next lower ranks to be seated on either side of the principle person. However, if the place of honour is allocated to a guest, then the host will sit directly opposite the honoured guest. The lowest ranking person will sit at the end of the table with their back to the door.

On my early trips to Japan, I was fascinated by the farewells. Whether after a visit to a shop, a restaurant or a hotel, the staff would bow and wave from the door until the guest was out of sight. One particular memory involves a group of around 150 Europeans on a visit to Kyoto. As the group departed in three coach buses, about twenty members of the hotel staff stood in a row outside the front door waving the guests off. Later that same day, as our plane was pulling away from the airport terminal, I looked out the window and noticed the ground crew all lined up, each at exactly the same distance from the other, waving off the aircraft and its passengers.

In spite of its complexities, some Japanese behaviour is a delight to experience and should be appreciated for what it is – a code of conduct rooted in respect for the guest and governed by rigid, unchanging rules of a tiered society.

Work Environment

The most visible difference between European and Japanese working environments is undoubtedly the open plan office. When I first moved to Brussels as a general manager, it was very difficult to adjust to having desks on either side of me as well as in front of me. I had been

17

used to my private office with a meeting table, and my direct reports also had small, but private offices.

On my early visits to the Tokyo headquarters, I was appalled to see the teams working in confined open plan offices. A team leader had a desk with his back to the wall. His team occupied a row of desks extending perpendicularly in front of him. The actual desk size for each individual was the smallest size imaginable, just accommodating a personal computer and some space for writing. Each desk was touching the desks on both sides of it, and also the desk facing it. A typical team would consist of eight or ten staff, five on the left side of the row and five on the right side. On my first visit to Tokyo in 1990, smoking in the office was still permitted, so half or more of these teams had ashtrays containing burning or recently extinguished cigarette stubs scattered over the desks. I am sure that the extra space that is permitted around each desk in Europe is considered by the Japanese to be a luxury. However, at least in Belgium, these things are governed by labour law so I wonder what working conditions Japanese companies would try to impose in European offices if these legal constraints were not enforced.

It is clear that Japanese companies make an effort to accommodate European preferences in this regard. Recently, there has been a move towards open plan offices in many European companies, but senior management enjoys the use of private offices. In Toyota Europe, only the level of vice president and above is afforded a private office, while in Bridgestone Europe only senior vice presidents and above get private offices. While most Europeans struggle to concentrate in this environment, they soon learn that one of the reasons the Japanese like it is because they can overhear what their staff members are discussing. This was always a comfort for the Japanese who usually do not trust their non-Japanese staff.

The theory is that if you need to have a confidential meeting or discussion, then you should use one of the many meeting rooms that are provided. However, in an office with more than 300 staff with a constant stream of visitors, there are never enough meeting rooms and it is almost impossible to book a meeting room with less than a week's notice. I have had many personal experiences of receiving important confidential phone calls for which there was no choice but to continue the conversation within earshot of several people. Other senior European managers had similar experiences with the result that confidential information was leaked.

Every Japanese manager with whom I discussed this topic could not quite accept that it was a problem; every European considered it dangerous and felt that it contributed to an overall poor working environment.

It is little wonder that the staff turnover at our European headquarters was high. At more than 20% annual turnover of staff, the company was running at more than double the rate of the Belgian market. There are several other contributing factors which I will address, but the open plan office definitely is one of them.

Working Hours

Another significant difference between European and Japanese working conditions is the number of working hours. While all the working contracts for European staff mention 37.5 hours, the unwritten expectation is that staff should work much longer. I must confess that I did not work as long as many others, but fifty hours a week from 08:30 until 07:30 was a typical working week for me, unless there was travel involved in which case early morning and late evening flights were the norm.

Most Europeans already know the Japanese reputation of working long hours. My surprise was how they used the "after hours". It was quite common to see Japanese colleagues using this time for networking. They would typically adopt a different demeanour from their office "persona" and visit each other to discuss issues in a casual manner. In many ways, it was the equivalent of the European's exchanges at the water fountain or coffee machine.

I talked with several Japanese colleagues about their late working hours and the conclusion was something like this: they are convinced that they cannot make a good impression with their boss or with senior managers by leaving the office before nine o'clock in the evening. Japanese that join big Japanese corporations feel that they have a job for life, and indeed they usually do. They feel indebted to the company and are willing to make sacrifices in their personal lives to give something back. This attitude also drives their willingness to give up their vacation time. It was quite common for my Japanese colleagues to forego most of their three weeks of holidays and to only take public holidays with an occasional day tagged on to a long weekend.

A business colleague who was once assigned to work in Japan for one of the other big global tyre companies, told me about his first day at work there. He had been introduced to his sales and marketing team, and settled into his desk at the head of the open plan office. At the end of the official finishing time, he noticed that none of the team had left, so he was embarrassed to leave. An hour later, still no one had left. Finally, he called aside one of his lieutenants to ask at what time the employees would leave. "Oh," he replied, "they are waiting for you to leave before they do".

Behave like the Japanese - Fall on your Sword.

Japanese Managers generally believe that Japanese values should be understood and accepted by European employees. One even proclaimed that if Europeans could not behave in the Japanese way, they should not be working for a Japanese company.

One year, when our subsidiary company in United Kingdom had failed to make the budgeted profit, the senior vice president of sales, proposed that the sales directors in United Kingdom should give up their company BMW cars and move to smaller more modest cars. He said this sacrifice would be a signal to the rest of the staff that they were experiencing hard times, and would set an example of cost saving and self-sacrifice. The managing director of the United Kingdom subsidiary tried to explain that the BMW cars the directors were driving were commensurate with the market level for their job. He warned that if they were forced to downgrade, then there was at risk of losing some of them, particularly the better ones.

The senior vice president was furious that his idea should be challenged, and replied that Joe, who happened to be the managing director, should be the first to set the example and show his commitment to saving money. Joe, finding himself in an impossible position, asked the director of finance and administration to study the cost/benefit of acting as he had been instructed. Unsurprisingly, the analysis revealed that as the cars were all on lease agreements, there would be large penalties for returning them early. These penalties were so severe that the cost to the company of downgrading the company cars would be close to 20,000 pounds. Believing that he now had a good argument to justify his position, Joe explained the analysis to his superior who refused to listen. He shouted at him to proceed as instructed and did not permit further discussion. Joe came to me to seek support. I recognised the validity of his argument and decided to raise it with the senior vice president when I found the right moment. When I did, he explained that the issue was not financial cost but sacrifice. He wanted the sales directors in the United Kingdom to make a sacrifice that would testify to their commitment to the company. In other words, he wanted them to fall on their swords and act in the Japanese way.

When Unaji arrived in Europe, one of the Scandinavian sales companies in the group had already begun a sales campaign linked to the Olympic Games in Sydney, to be held in 2000. They had designed an elaborate points system, whereby their dealers could accumulate points through their purchases, and over a three-year period earn a trip to the Olympic Games in Sydney. The campaign had been launched at a series of dealer meetings, and many dealers had signed up to it. With less than two years left to run in the campaign, Unaji announced that he was not in favour of the campaign, and explained that three years duration was too long and it should be cancelled. Once again, several people tried to explain that it was not feasible to cancel the program at this advanced stage. Once again, he was unwilling to discuss the subject or listen to reason. He kept re-iterating his dislike for the three- year program and that it was to be stopped. In this case, the consequences of cancellation would have ruined our business in that country as well as the reputations of the management of the subsidiary. The case was so serious that the company managers were willing to resign rather than to cancel the project. In the end, the campaign continued, but was never referred to in presentations or reports to the headquarters. In fact, over time, Unaji seemed to forget about it or perhaps believed that it had actually been cancelled. Under his regime, one of the only ways people who worked under him could manage was to pretend that things were different from what they really were. Those who understood this early enough and learned to report only what Unaji wanted to hear, were, interestingly enough, the more successful in their careers.

On another occasion, Unaji was visiting the Information Technology (IT) department in the building. This was a rare event as IT was not in his area of responsibility. As he toured, he noticed that several of the desks had shelves attached to them for staff to store papers, files and equipment. The shelving increased the space between desks and created more private work space. It was a benefit the employees appreciated, but one which Unaji denounced as a violation of the open plan office. He instructed the head of IT to immediately remove the shelves from every desk. The head of IT, a European, objected, not least because Unaji was not his boss. But Unaji was a very senior executive and felt his word was law. A standoff ensued; Unaji left but not before he had made perfectly clear what he expected. The head of IT, who had stood up to Unaji declared that he had no intention of following the instruction. In fact, he would respect the wishes of the employees and create slightly more private working space. There was little further reference to the incident, and Unaji was repatriated to Japan soon after. A few years later, I realised that the shelves were gone. I never learned what happened. I believe it was a gradual process. As desks or people moved around or as new people joined the department, one by one the shelves disappeared. I am sure that some Japanese members in the department were told they had to make sure that Unaji's instructions were carried out, and it was done with the least possible loss of face for the IT manager.

This inability to understand that non-Japanese personnel are not likely to act like Japanese ultimately contributed to the lack of success of the company. It is not a question of which business culture is better or worse; it is a question of respect for the diversity within a company. This requires training for both cultures. Inter-cultural understanding was unfortunately lacking at Bridgestone.

Reporting Lines for Overseas Japanese

When Japanese graduates join a corporation, they assume a lifetime commitment from both sides. With very few exceptions, that is exactly how it works out. This means that when Japanese employees are posted to overseas positions in the United States or Europe, they know that it is a temporary posting and that they will be repatriated to Japan at some stage, normally after about three years. With the assurance that they have job security, they feel free to challenge their European counterparts and, if they feel it necessary, to withdraw their support from their European boss if they have one.

Over the years, as one of the senior European managers, I had several Japanese direct reports on my team. At one stage, as vice president of sales and marketing for Europe, four of my five direct reports were Japanese. The most extraordinary factor was that I was never part of the selection process for their positions. Furthermore, the evaluation of their performance was done by the Human Resources department in Japan with no input from me. Invariably, each year, I would be informed that one of the directors was being re-assigned in the group and that a person completely unknown to me would be replacing him.

Kazuo Namiki writes that,[2] "Senior Japanese executives assigned abroad are usually in their mid-forties or early fifties. Prior to overseas assignments, they usually are only section chiefs or department heads at the home office. In overseas ventures, they are assigned to top management positions and given titles such as chief executive officer, president, senior vice president, and general manager. Some of the senior managers are *amakudari,* descending to an overseas subsidiary from "heaven" the home office. They are often sent down because suitable managerial positions are not available to them in Japan. They are assigned to top overseas positions not necessarily because of their exceptional professional competency, but because of their extensive personal ties with many key people at the home office. They may also have public relations skills considered convenient for entertaining important clients who will visit from Japan. In fact, those who are in their mid-fifties are given titular positions in overseas subsidiaries before their retirement as a reward for their many years of dedicated service." Consequently, even senior managers working for overseas subsidiaries do not have the same authority and influence that their colleagues in Japan with similar managerial titles may have. In short, the overseas Japanese multinationals are neither autonomous nor semi-autonomous operations, but are locked into a tight hierarchical relationship with their parent companies.

---

[2] Doing Business with Japan, 2000, Kazuo Namiki, Page 161

This was certainly true of Bridgestone Europe. When I was in charge of sales and marketing for Europe, a new director position was created under me, and was filled by the celebrated older Japanese, Nakajima, who had only three years left before his retirement. In reality, he was an old friend and colleague of the CEO in Europe at the time. This arrangement allowed the two to travel and socialise together. It was made clear to me that Nakajima could set his own work objectives. His travel plans, although under my budget control, were not to be questioned. Any interference with him would be considered as direct interference with the CEO.

Handle with Care

I had some excellent supportive Japanese colleagues, but I also had some appointees who made it patently clear that they would work independently from me. For many Europeans in similar positions to mine, this situation was untenable. My choice was to work with those that I could work with, and to allow the independent rebels to have their way on most subjects. I only stepped in when critically important strategic issues were on the table. Inevitably, this required a high level of diplomacy. Confronting a Japanese colleague directly and instructing him to do something is guaranteed to fail, and even worse, can lead to long-term friction. Before I could change the mind-set of one of my Japanese directors, I had to be absolutely convinced that my position was accurate, and then to begin the process of *nemawashi* or internal selling with other Japanese decision makers, who often included the Japanese CEO.

One of my European colleagues, George, also a vice president, had two Japanese members on his team. With one he had repeated difficulties. Shinohara-san did not speak English well, and took care of his business responsibilities with little discussion or approval from his vice president. One day, the CEO who socialised a lot with Shinohara-san came to George and proposed that Shinohara should be promoted to a director level. It was very unusual for the CEO to discuss ideas like this with his European vice president, but Mizutani was one of the more respectful CEOs. George should have accepted the proposal of the CEO; instead he shared his real assessment of Shinohara and advised strongly against the promotion.

To my surprise at the time, Mizutani accepted George's view and did not pursue the promotion. However, the incident set in motion a chain of events that led to George's dismissal from the company a year later. George's objection derailed Shinohara's career planning who was reassigned soon afterwards. Shinohara's reassignment was from a general manager level and not from a director level, and this had career development consequences for him, but also for George. Shinohara's replacement who reported to George, came into the European organisation knowing about the "Shinohara story" and therefore arrived with prejudice against George. He regularly bypassed George to report to George's boss, who was also a newly appointed CEO. A few months later, George was dismissed.

Us and Them – No Other Opinions Required

It was difficult for me to believe that the reporting structure in such a big company could be so mismanaged. It is critical for successful management to appoint the best people to key positions and for the chain of command to be clear. Excluding European bosses from the selection of the Japanese team members for their own team led to mistrust, and gave the Japanese staff the security of "a job for life". Meanwhile, their European counterparts felt that they were always at risk and that they were constantly battling with an unbalanced and unfair power shift. This was, of course, a dysfunctional context in which to work because it implied that personnel from non-Japanese countries would not be treated the same way as their Japanese colleagues. This is not a recipe for success.

The Japanese include respect for diversity as one of their social responsibility objectives. What I have concluded is that they respect the differences between Muslims and Jews, Africans and Europeans, but they have not considered the differences between Japanese and everyone else. The rules that they apply for themselves do not necessarily apply to non-Japanese employees.

The different rules for Japanese and non-Japanese can be interpreted as unfair by either group depending on the issue. For several years, mid-level Japanese staff members in the Brussels office of the European organisation, unlike their European counterparts, were not entitled to a company car. The concept of fairness differs enormously between the East and the West, and therefore it is necessary for companies to address those differences if they want their organisation to function. Ignoring the differences and the feelings of unfairness on both sides can only lead to demotivation.

In Bridgestone Europe, there was an Executive Management Committee (EMC). This committee met twice a month to discuss topics and proposals from different divisions and to reach a consensus or decision about them. Of course if one had an important project to bring to EMC, the *nemawashi* process would have been instigated already. Under the chairmanship of my last Japanese CEO, Shimbashi, the whole concept of the EMC became a farce because his management style was nothing less than dictatorial. The members quickly learned that any interjection not fully in line with the opinion of the CEO was likely to be shot down in an insulting manner. I had some difficulty accepting that my input was not wanted, especially on topics where I had vast experience and knowledge.

Shimbashi remained in his position of CEO in Europe for only eighteen months. He made some excellent business decisions and implemented effective business processes, but his autocratic style impeded debate and collaborative or innovative thinking. Shimbashi regularly gave his opinion about presentations and then invariably looked around the table and asked for "any other opinions." It was comical to watch the body language around the table: eyes dropped; everyone was suddenly "deep in thought ", and final various forms of nodding were offered as if to say "Hmm, when I deeply consider this issue I see that the opinion of Shimbashi is indeed correct, and I support it".

Use and Abuse

Some of my European colleagues were of the opinion that "bad" treatment of employees was reserved for the non-Japanese. I disagree because the fact is that some of my high level Japanese colleagues were also unreasonably abused and their unwavering loyalty was taken advantage of. Kobayashi was one of them.

Kobayashi, who worked on my team in Brussels for a number of years, was asked to return to Japan to take up a new position. He appealed against the move arguing that one of his daughters was at a critical phase in her education and that she only had one and a half years before completing her high school diploma. He was told that he could move as had been requested or he could leave the company. He asked for financial assistance to keep his daughter in Brussels to finish her course. This was also refused. Finally, he returned to Japan alone, leaving his wife and two daughters in Belgium at his own expense. At the end of eighteen months, as his family prepared to return to Tokyo to join Kobayashi and for his daughter to attend university in Tokyo, Kobayashi was informed that he had to move again. This time he had to go to Shanghai. The next stage of his daughter's education was already arranged in Tokyo, and so Kobayashi enjoyed an overlap of one week with his family before he had to take up his position in Shanghai. At least it was feasible to travel from Shanghai to Tokyo at weekends from time to time. But two years later, Kobayashi was transferred to Europe again. Once again he was alone.

Loyalty repaid?

Japanese employees are at risk of being taken advantage of because of their loyalty. In 1999, at a time when Bridgestone was going through a period of corporate restructuring, positions of "foreigners" at the Tokyo head office were eliminated and training programs for foreign employees were cancelled. At the same time, Japanese employees, many of whom had dedicated their careers to their company were affected. Some like Masaharu Nonaka chose to protest in the most extreme way: he committed Hara-Kiri (a violent form of suicide) in the office of the President.

[3]*Moments before he slashed his stomach with a 14-inch fish-slicing knife today, a 58-year-old manager in a business suit was in heated talks over corporate restructuring with the president of one of the world's largest tire makers and said he would commit ritual suicide.*

Masaharu Nonaka, who was a manager at Bridgestone Corporation until 1992, was working at an affiliate and had been asked to step down as manager in charge of purchasing golf equipment, according to Japanese news reports.

Bridgestone, based in Japan, has been in the process of corporate restructuring, and since 1993 it has nudged more than 2,000

---

[3] New York Times, Mar 24 1999,Sheryll WuDunn

employees off the payrolls, leaving 13,000.

Mr. Nonaka's case strikes a strong chord in Japan, which is suffering from record unemployment and recession. Few workers have vented their frustrations by taking their own lives, and Mr. Nonaka, who leaves a wife and two grown daughters, is certainly an extreme case. But his suicide underscores the psychological distress that workers, managers and their families are undergoing as the country struggles to revive and restructure its economy.

"It's a kind of performance," said Hiroyoshi Ishikawa, a professor of social psychology at Seijo University. "It's a kind of protest to the company policy of restructuring."

In modern Japan, hara-kiri, or seppuku, is almost entirely the stuff of Kabuki drama, and Mr. Nonaka's violent suicide is not seen as a sign of a grisly trend. But ritual disembowelment was part of a rigid code in which samurai warriors killed themselves by sinking their swords diagonally across their stomachs to avoid disgrace, dishonor and the indignity of defeat.

When the Meiji Emperor died in 1912, Gen. Maresuke Nogi, a hero in the Russo-Japanese war, committed seppuku, killing his wife along with himself.

Today, in a discussion that lasted about an hour in the executive offices with Yoichiro Kaizaki, Bridgestone's president, Mr. Nonaka had submitted a letter of complaint about the company's policies on retirement and resignation, the police said.

Suddenly Mr. Nonaka became very agitated. He stripped off his clothes to the waist, took out a pair of knives and screamed that he was going to commit hara-kiri.

Before arriving at the President's office that day, Nonaka had taken the time to contact the media. Journalists arrived at the head office just as the emergency services were taking Nonaka away on a stretcher.

Extreme displays of frustration such as Nonaka's are rare, but they underline the essential difference between Japanese and westerners: Japanese employees are more likely to be torn by the conflict that arises from the demands of loyalty to their employer that is tested by the harsh treatment they may receive.

Constant training of employees has become a normal part of managing a workforce, at least in Europe. Blue collar and white collar employees can nowadays expect regular updating and training during their career.

At Bridgestone, I watched a new training program being prepared for factory workers. The program was a part of a global training project being driven from the Japanese headquarters. I observed a section where a number of Japanese training principles were translated into English. I was astonished to read, "Scold first, praise later". I must admit to a management style that emphasises coaching, mentoring, sharing a vision, and avoiding open conflict unless absolutely necessary. "Scold first, Praise later" appears to reflect a military style, which I do not believe is effective in Europe today, and certainly explains in part the high staff turnover.

Terrorised to Breaking Point

The monthly sales meetings were dreaded by visiting managers. One managing director, Eirik, was taken ill while travelling to a monthly sales meeting from a Scandinavian country. He called ahead to say that he could not attend. Eirik's doctor called it a nervous breakdown, and ordered him off work for several months. In fact, Eirik, in his early forties never worked again. Yet, his CEO called him and accused him of being weak and afraid to face the difficult meeting.

On another occasion, I was standing in the toilet preparing myself for a long meeting and chatting to Mizutani, the CEO at the time. While we stood there, the door burst open and in ran the Japanese deputy from United Kingdom, Sekiguchi. As he stumbled past us, with hand over mouth, his loud retching noises could not be disguised. He never made it to the toilet bowl. Mizutani and I both looked on with concern but we had already understood what was happening. We were in the count down to the sales meeting at which Sekiguchi would have to present his market performance for the previous month. The meeting would be chaired by the infamous Unaji. We all expected that blood would be spilled, and everyone, including Sekiguchi, would be silently comparing the meetings to the last moments before an execution.

Sekiguchi, cleaned himself up, went back into the meeting room and did his job. I was left to reflect on how his mental state could make him so terrified that he could be made physically ill.

Unaji told me once that he did not single out the non-Japanese for hard treatment. He proudly confided that he used the same abusive methods with all employees. The truth is that there were instances when some Japanese did get worse treatment than non-Japanese and my belief that we were all on the same team was severely tested

Know your place

A young Japanese trainee was dispatched from Tokyo to my department without any consultation with the European management or with Unaji who was furious that he had not been consulted. For several weeks, he refused to meet with or acknowledge the new junior trainee, Hamada. Hamada was very uncomfortable when Unaji would talk to everyone in his area of the office except him. Despite numerous efforts to change this, Unaji ignored him.

Several weeks later, Unaji invited Hamada to join a group of Japanese for dinner that evening. He even suggested that Hamada should come to Unaji's apartment for a drink before the dinner so that he could get to know him better. Hamada was terrified but he accepted and turned up at Unaji's apartment. Unaji and his small dog were the only occupants of the apartment that evening. Hamada sat on a low couch opposite a low coffee table; the small dog sat beside him and stared up at him. Unaji returned from the kitchen with a glass of beer for Hamada and sat down opposite him. Hamada listened intently while Unaji spoke, but then he noticed that the dog was drinking from his glass of beer. He flashed a glance at Unaji, who was watching. Unaji said nothing; he stared back challengingly. Hamada reached for the glass.

Unaji raised his glass and said *"kampai"*, the Japanese equivalent to "cheers", and drank from his own glass. Hamada gave a slight bow and drank from his. Unaji grinned. The message was clear: the hierarchy was affirmed. By drinking from the same glass as the dog, Hamada had accepted that he was at the level of Unaji's dog. From that day on, Hamada was treated like the rest of the staff. But for him, anything was better than being ignored.

A Rare Gesture to the Europeans

The Europeans in the company fully understood that Mizutani, who had extended his stay in Europe by one year, would retire and return to Japan within a few months. His heir apparent, Unaji, was already planning a huge "kick off" meeting for the following year which would mark his accession to the position of CEO and President of the European organisation.

Unbeknownst to me and to my European colleagues, Mizutani had realised that Unaji was not the best choice to replace him as CEO and set about changing plans that were already in place. During his end of year visit to Tokyo, he arranged to meet with the global CEO to explain his position and to propose an alternative plan. His suggestion was rejected. To his great credit Mizutani set about a process of *nemawashi* with the other board members to convince them of his new plan and to gain their support. Over the course of a week he garnered sufficient support to return to the global CEO and to convince him to reconsider his initial decision. In the end, he succeeded. Over the following weeks, the news broke and the Europeans who had survived the preceding three years celebrated. Instead of the dark days we had been anticipating nervously, we actually entered one of the most successful periods of the company.

Single minded disrespect

Some years after Mizutani had ensured Unaji's return to Japan and the organisation had recovered from the damage he had caused, Nimbashi arrived. He had come through the technical side of the business and had done great work with product development and product evaluation. His move to Brussels was a step into business management and real commercial life. He was a director reporting to me. I was glad to have such a knowledgeable product-oriented expert on my team and looked forward to working with him. My optimism was short-lived.

Almost from the start, he developed direct communications with my boss, a Japanese CEO called Mori. One easily underestimates the advantage that Japanese managers have as a result of their networks. While a European manager can have difficulty finding time to meet face to face with his CEO because of the CEO's busy schedule, the lower-ranked Japanese mix in the same social circles. They are drinking together, eating together, and attending the same parties and golf competitions. The power of this network gives them a huge advantage over their European counterparts.

Nimbashi would convince Mori of an idea he wanted to pursue, would receive informal approval, and would proceed, often without even informing me who happened to be his boss. When I questioned him, Nimbashi would reply that he had received his instructions directly from the CEO. It was frustrating to find myself outside the communication loop in these cases. Oddly enough, I could accept – albeit reluctantly - Nimbashi's methods as part of the culture of a Japanese company. I had greater difficulty accepting that Mori, to whom I was reporting, was allowing and even encouraging this kind of exclusion of his European managers.

Excluding European managers from the communication loop was common practice throughout my fifteen years in the Brussels office, but during Mori's time it was at its worst. Mori, who had been pulled out of North America during a crisis caused by a product recall, had been appointed as European CEO at a time when there were very few Japanese candidates for the job. He was totally unsuitable for the job, and within eighteen months had transformed the company result from healthy to disastrous. There was no economic crisis to blame; he was simply incompetent

Hide that Incompetence

On one occasion, we were hosting a dinner for an important visiting business partner and his wife. There were four couples, Mori and his wife, a Japanese deputy and his wife, my wife and I, and our guest and his wife. The magnificent table was circular and our visitor sat directly facing Mori whose wife sat to his side. Mori's social skills were poor and it was tough work keeping the conversation lively and interesting. At one point, as our guest was recounting a true story, a look of utter surprise crossed his face. Almost immediately, I noticed that Mori had fallen asleep. We knew that Mori could sleep anywhere, anytime but this was quite astounding. Mori's wife had also noticed what had happened and gave him a well- practiced elbow to the ribs which jolted him awake. He had, however, missed the story and could think of nothing to say. Fortunately, our guest was not insulted but concerned. He later asked me if Mori was sick or on medication.

To his credit, Mori seemed to know that he was incompetent. After six months in Europe, he decided that he needed to appoint a strong number two to be the tough guy. His choice for senior vice president was a European who was almost at retirement age and well-known for his autocratic management style. In fact, he earned his nickname of Rottweiler. We used to joke about the CEO getting a new Rottweiler. Over time, it became clear that Mori had made another very serious mistake; he had failed to keep his Rottweiler on a tight chain. He did not oversee his decisions or behaviour but allowed him to run wild while he slept in his office. It was not long before the Rottweiler decided that I should be reassigned to another area of responsibility.

Meanwhile, Mori's appointment delivered his presentations to top management with the emphasis on what the Japanese wanted to hear. Whether the report was true or not was of little importance. If it was what the top management wanted to hear, that was what he told them. He could report a catastrophic event in such a way that it could have been mistaken for a success. On one occasion, he was forced to take over a bankrupt company but convinced the Japanese management that he had made an excellent low-cost investment. That it was actually a huge cost for a loss-making company was understood by others among us but it was not until several years later when the senior vice president had retired and all the Japanese managers had been re-assigned, that new management invested several more millions to shut down the loss making acquisition.

Ruling by Fear

Meanwhile, Nimbashi flourished in this environment, and even adopted the Rottweiler style with his own team. He had a particular dislike for the women in his team. He did not rate Europeans, and he did not value women. When the two came together in the form of a European female, they were there to be abused. He was used to the practice of Tokyo office where the lowest level female employees were identified by their black aprons. Their job was to fetch and serve the coffee, water and lunches for their superiors and to perform administrative tasks like photo copying, mailing etc. Around this time, a book called *Fear and Trembling* by Amelie Nothomb was published. Written by the daughter of a former Belgian Ambassador to Japan where she was born, it told the story of her experiences working for a year in a Japanese corporation in Tokyo. The book was widely reviewed in Belgium, and every Belgian working for a Japanese company read it. So did members of Nimbashi's team. For them, Nothomb's story was the story of their own experience working under Nimbashi. Like her, public humiliation and abuse in front of colleagues was common place. That which was almost never seen in Western companies was a regular occurrence for Nimbashi's staff and, incidentally, the subject of much of the coffee machine discussion.

Nimbashi presided over the unhappiest team I have ever seen. He focused on giving Mori what Mori wanted, but in Japan it was becoming very clear that Mori was leading the company towards disaster. Nimbashi was judged as having failed; was transferred and reassigned, and has remained off the radar ever since.

Learning From the Past.

Learning lessons from the past can be hugely important for any company. A former human resources colleague, Michel Gombert, once told me that, "Organisations don't have memories, only the people in them have". It reminded me of a quote from the 19th century German philosopher, Freidrich Hegel, "The only thing we learn from history is that we never learn anything from history"

In an organisation like Bridgestone Europe, where upper management was frequently changed, a piece of valuable experience left with every one of them. This does not mean that people cannot be moved or replaced, but it is important to keep a balance between new blood and new ideas on the one hand, and experience and knowledge on the other.

Perhaps, the Japanese management felt that they had enough knowledge and experience in the Tokyo head office, but it was a very different picture on the ground in Europe. I know many aging executives in many companies who moan about attending meetings where the latest young enthusiastic whizz kid is putting his ground-breaking idea on the table. The executive is holding his tongue thinking, "Yes indeed, we tried that fifteen years ago and found out that it doesn't work because……" Not wanting to be perceived as negative, he keeps quiet, and watches as the course of action is implemented and fails.

There is a difference between resistance to change and bringing the fruits of experience, even negative, to bear in discussions. Change is necessary and most good businessmen either lead or support change. The weakness is when the lessons of the past are not considered in the change plans.

The Japanese, however, take "forgetting the past" to a new level. They often celebrate any idea as a new one, and they just as often dismiss experience and knowledge from the past, at least if it is the experience and knowledge of a "local". I saw far too many cases where valuable experience was ignored.

Why Can't Europeans Think More Like the Japanese?

"To foster a workplace environment in which employees feel motivated and take joy in their work" was one of the stated objectives of Bridgestone's CSR policy.

The staff turnover at the European headquarters averaged around 20%, except for the period immediately following the economic crash in 2008/9. This figure alone is an indication of the lack of job satisfaction among the employees. The human resources department offered piecemeal ideas that might improve the working environment. For example, the dress code was changed to declare that men only needed to wear a tie if they had a meeting with someone from outside the company, but for internal meetings they could wear an open collar. Then to really motivate people, a "casual Friday" was introduced when employees could wear jeans and T-shirts unless, once again, there was a meeting with an outside visitor. But the casual Friday was limited to the summer months and the week between Christmas and New Year. The Japanese management actually believed that these concessions would help the morale of the employees and increase their motivation.

For those of us that had regular contact with our colleagues in Bridgestone North America, we knew that their dress code was casual every day, and that they came to work in chinos and polo shirts. We were equally aware that in the Tokyo head office the employees all wore dark suits and white shirts with ties every day. An exception to the official dress code allowed Japanese members to wear a company jacket instead of a formal jacket particularly in the plants or in the research and development departments where there were few visitors. These jackets were not available for non-Japanese employees, and were usually brought to Europe by individual employees. The wearers could differentiate themselves from the local employees. The unspoken message that they brought was "I am from the engine room of the company. I know information from the inside that you will never know". These differences across the globe, underlined the cultural differences that Bridgestone needed to grapple with, but failed to, at least in Europe.

Flexi time and home working gradually became popular in European companies, but not in Bridgestone. The in-built practice of working long hours in the office made working from home analogous to taking the day off. Working from home was neither encouraged nor allowed, unless an employee was sick. The company continued to lag behind the European standard behaviour by more than ten years.

Time to Re-analyse the Analysis

The company maintained a well-staffed Human Resources department, which had grown more than any other department. One of its projects was an employee satisfaction survey. The internal objective under the ISO 9000 certification demanded that the survey be carried out every two years. Results of the first two surveys showed that the level of morale was declining: the most recent change of CEO had been a disaster; headcount turnover was as its highest ever, and morale was at its lowest.

The top management took the decision not to publish the results among the employees. Admitting to failure was never a realistic option. Even though employees eagerly awaited the employee satisfaction survey because it provided an opportunity to give feedback to the top, express their current feelings and frustrations, top management decided that the best course of action was to postpone the survey. The management preferred to risk non-compliance with an audit than to publish a negative result from an employee survey.

It was another two years before the survey was reintroduced, by which time more than half the employees from four years earlier had left the company, and the CEO had been changed twice. Effectively, the survey results could not be compared and they were used in a way that focussed on the future rather than making comparisons with the past. More energy was spent on preparing for surveys than dealing with the actual points of dissatisfaction identified by the employees.

A brilliant book called *People Follow You* by Jeb Blount recognises this as common practice in companies. He notes that,

[4]"It has always disturbed me how organisations will put into place elaborate (and often expensive) incentive systems designed at improving employee retention and productivity. Yet, other than lip service, are unwilling to hold their leaders accountable for employee satisfaction and retention. How many companies as part of their review system assess the emotional impact leaders have on their people? [..]How many companies teach leaders interpersonal leadership skills? Not many."

If this is how Blount evaluates companies in America, consider the additional complexities that are introduced in an intercultural setting.

---

[4] People Follow You. Jeb Blount. December 2011. page 7.

Chapter 2

Trust

Freedom to Act – Genbutsu Genba- Analysis- Consensus

Japanese managers inherently distrust their non-Japanese employees. This trait has significant consequences, and both Japanese and non-Japanese have to use all their powers and skills to overcome it. Distrust is such a deeply rooted problem that it is unlikely to be overcome for several generations, if ever.

Trust and Consensus

Japanese managers demand verifiable data and facts. There are two important reasons for this. First, the manager's language proficiency is generally poor, so by developing the discussion with reference to data makes it easier for them to follow the arguments. Second, it takes a long time to earn the trust of a Japanese manager. Often, even before they arrive in Europe, they have already internalized the notion that they should never accept what they are told by the locals.

One of their workplace principles is *Genbutsu Genba*, or "Decision making based on verified on-site observations". Because the process of explaining complex issues to a Japanese manager is persistently more difficult for Europeans than for their Japanese colleagues, it is often prudent to assure the support of a junior or same-level Japanese colleague to help provide the explanations to the manager. But, even when the argumentation is supported by a Japanese colleague, one should assume that there will be resistance. Reluctance to taking responsibility for decisions is inherent to Japanese management practice.

Towards the end of my time at Bridgestone, one of my colleagues shared the following story with me. It appears that my colleague's CEO had insisted that he would be the final decision-maker for business contracts that went beyond a pre-established value. The Fleet

Management division had been preparing a bid for a major contract and, after a lengthy process, had convinced its director and senior vice president, both Japanese, that the bid they were putting forward was viable. Nevertheless for the bid to go ahead, the sign off from the CEO was required. A meeting was called. Four people from the department, including the senior vice president and the director, both of whom were Japanese, met with the CEO and using an extensive number of spreadsheets, explained the deal to him in great detail. At the end of the presentation, the CEO said, "Good, this looks fine to me. So if my senior vice president and director are ready to accept responsibility and sign it off, then I will sign off too." He then turned and looked at the senior vice president. Suddenly the atmosphere changed: the senior vice president cleared his throat loudly and nervously, shuffled his feet uncomfortably, breathed deeply and took his hands off the table. All signs of extreme discomfort and an unwillingness to sign. Since the CEO was unwilling to take sole responsibility, the approval form was not signed and the deadline for submitting the tender was not met.

This unwillingness to make decisions can be very frustrating for European staff members because it often results in lost business opportunities. However, it should also be said that it can often prove to be a very effective strategy to avoid making poor decisions. In my time at Bridgestone, few bad decisions were actually made. All issues, all data, all facts were analysed, re-analysed and studied deeply. I never saw a manager hurry toward a decision that would be regretted later.

Japanese decision-making is governed by a process called "nemawashi". Europeans need to understand this process if they want to succeed in a Japanese company. Nobody taught me; I had to discover it for myself.

"Many people who do business with or work for Japanese companies are familiar with the term nemawashi, which refers to a commonly-used Japanese consensus building technique. It's often said that doing nemawashi is essential in order to get a decision made or changes implemented in a Japanese organisation. However, how exactly does one do nemawashi?

First, let's recall the key characteristics of *nemawashi*. First, it's typically done as a more low-key alternative to the standard western style meeting filled with debate and clashing positions. It involves conversations, either one-on-one or in very small groups, to avoid the public display of differences of opinion. And its goal is persuasion.

Nemawashi typically begins when the person who is promoting a particular proposal or course of action seeks out those he believes will be key decision-makers. This is not always easy in a Japanese company, as many people weigh in on each decision and it's not necessary clear whose voice will carry more weight. So, generally to be safe a good *nemawashi*-er will do several *nemawashi* meetings each with a small subset of people, until they have methodically covered all the likely key influencers.

The *nemawashi* meeting itself may be either formal or informal. At one extreme, it could be buttonholing someone in the hallway or elevator, or stopping by their desk to chat. Along the lines of "By the way, I wanted to tell you about something I've been working on...." It could be brought up casually over a semi-social occasion such as lunch or dinner or drinks or while playing golf. Or, it could be an explicitly-planned meeting specifically for the purpose of discussing the topic.

One very formal type of nemawashi is the "pre-meeting", which takes place before a larger more structured meeting. In a pre-meeting, any issues planned for discussion in the larger meeting that might prove to be controversial are hashed out ahead of time so that they don't create embarrassing snags. Any new ideas or proposals that are going to be presented can be floated in the pre-meeting, in order to avoid any surprises during the main meeting.

The key point of the *nemawashi* encounter is to explain the plan or proposal or idea that you are promoting, and getting the reaction of the person(s) you are doing *nemawashi* with. Do they completely hate it? Like some parts and not others? Do they have specific suggestions for improving it, or improving the chances that it will be accepted?

Based on the feedback from your *nemawashi* meeting, you'll want to refine your course of action. If an important person is showing strong resistance, you may want to abandon the idea or give it a complete reworking. You may have gotten other ideas for polishing the concept, or even suggestions for others to do *nemawashi* with. After an iterative process of successive *nemawashi* meetings and refinements to your plan, you'll either have something sure to succeed, or will understand why your idea is unlikely to be approved." [5]

It is no wonder then that decision-making takes so long in a Japanese company. An additional challenge for Europeans in this process is that it is more difficult for them than for Japanese to get actual face-to-face time with the people who are a part of the crucial decision-making process.

One colleague found a strategy to overcome this barrier. He realised that the CEO was relaxed and had his guard down when he was on one of his several breaks in the smoking room. So he took up smoking and timed his smoking breaks to coincide with those of the CEO. This strategy gave him unprecedented insight into the thoughts of the CEO, and a rare opportunity to impress the CEO with his views about what needed to be done. Within a year, he was promoted.

Another idiosyncrasy that took me a long time to understand was the Japanese reluctance to say "no". In my early days, I assumed that my proposals were still under consideration because nobody had actually said no to them. Later, I understood that saying "no" outright is considered impolite and that the Japanese used it sparingly, if at all. One learned that if a manager or colleague began shifting in their seat or began mumbling uncomfortable responses that may have included, "Hmmm. Very difficult. Hmmm, I don't know", the answer was "NO WAY."

Guardians or Watchdogs

In each of the six main European markets, the Bridgestone sales company had a local managing director and a Japanese deputy whose main role was to watch and report on the actions of the managing director. The managing director was the person legally in charge of the company, but he could only survive if he checked every decision with his Japanese deputy. The deputy would use his connections in the

---

[5] Rochelle Kopp. A Nemawashi How to. May 2010.
http://www.japanintercultural.com

Japanese network of the company to ensure that any decision taken by the managing director was in line with the directions of the Japanese top management.

One failing of this approach, of course, was that very often, the hierarchy at headquarters was too far removed from local issues to be able to make a sound judgment. This repeatedly led to one of two outcomes: either approval was withheld and the managing director was informed that he should not proceed; or, and this was more likely, a deeper analysis that included more background information about the issue was requested. In the latter case, the data needed to be transformed into a presentation and delivered before a meeting with top managers.

Regional managing directors quickly learned that it was only worth preparing these presentations when the issue was critically important. Only these issues could justify the time and resources required to research and put such cases together. For all other day to day operating issues, they were forced to make the decisions themselves and, depending upon the relationship they had with their Japanese deputy, they would either conceal the issue from him or convince him to support it without reporting to the hierarchy. The success of the latter strategy depended on the deputy's pragmatism: those who focused solely on business operations would not report; those who focused on reporting lines would never decide anything without the approval of the hierarchy.

How Not to Make Things Happen!

In my early days of reporting directly to a Japanese boss, I knew nothing about the *nemawashi* process. I was a young ambitious executive in a hurry to make progress. Having set up the new Bridgestone subsidiary company in Ireland which was growing well, I was reporting to the managing director of Bridgestone UK who was Japanese. When he returned to Japan, he was replaced by Yasuka who was a very different kind of manager: he was much quieter and happy to give me the autonomy I needed to run the business in Ireland.

One of the business difficulties we had in Ireland at the time was the fact that Northern Ireland, as a part of the United Kingdom, was run as a part of the UK organisation. The market in the Republic of Ireland was run in its own currency, the Irish punt, while the Northern Ireland business was run in British pounds. Unfortunately, as the economies were quite different, the comparative value of the two currencies changed often, so a comparison of prices on either side of the border would show differences that could become significant and create *parallel imports*. When dealers took advantage of these price differences to buy on one side of the border and sell on the other, it created an unstable market and unfair competition.

Recognising this problem, I had the idea of changing the way we did business in Ireland so that just one organisation would manage the business on both sides of the border. This would enable better price management and lead to more stability. This was all taking place around the mid-nineties when Ireland was going through what was called, the Peace Process, during which it was hoped that the years of political instability were coming to an end. For the first time in hundreds of years, my idea of a single organisation managing the business on the whole island was actually feasible.

I presented my idea to Yasuka, and briefly explained where I saw the advantages for the company. His reaction was marked by his hesitation to take on another project, and since I did not have supporting charts and data to present to him, Yasuka dismissed my proposal. I decided that it would be a waste of time to try and discuss it further with him.

While this was going on, there was a flood of parallel imports coming from Northern Ireland because of the low value of the British pound, and it was becoming very difficult to run our business in the Republic of Ireland. I decided to bring my case to the European CEO, but this time I took care to prepare a thorough study and analysis to support my proposal. I had realised that his knowledge and understanding of Irish economics could only be rudimentary at best and that without my data to help him understand the situation, my efforts would be useless.

An analysis of the selling prices on either side of the border confirmed that the business was more profitable in the Republic. A further analysis of the distribution costs showed considerable potential savings from merging two warehouse facilities into one, and substantial economies of scale by harmonising the sales forces. The total potential benefit to the organisation was more than one million pounds; the business would grow steadily and become more stable.

On my next visit to Brussels, I sought out the European CEO and presented my proposal with the supporting analysis. The CEO, Imai, was impressed with the work and the idea, and set up a series of meetings with other Japanese senior management to approve it. I was invited to present the proposal to the management of Bridgestone UK which included my boss, Yasuka and the people in the United Kingdom responsible for the business in Northern Ireland. I presented to a very sceptical and unhappy audience, but I suspected that the decision had already been made by a more senior management team, and that my audience had little choice but to accept my proposal.

I was pleased with my achievement until Yasuka took me aside. He was very upset about the way I had handled the process. I had gone over his head without his knowledge and I had embarrassed him in the process. He had lost face before the European management team because when he had been asked for his opinion, he had been unable to support the idea because he did not know its details. I felt Yasuka's pain as he talked to me and his words brought me back down to earth. I had been too focused on the business result to take either the process or his personal position into account.

In my defence, I knew that it would have taken many more months of *nemawashi* to get him to support the idea before bringing it to a higher level, and I might even have failed to get the proposal through at all. Nevertheless, the bullish approach that I had taken is just not acceptable in a Japanese company. I was fortunate that Yasuka did not write me off after that incident. In fact, he was one of the main players in my move to the European headquarters two years later. It was a most important lesson for me.

I would advise any Japanese company working in Europe to carefully educate and coach their local employees about the importance of *nemawashi* and other common Japanese practices. During my career, I have noted with regret that this important training is neglected.

The Silent Treatment

Another practice which I only understood later in my career when I was involved in some very high-level negotiations was the practice of keeping silent. When I was authorised to meet with executives from Nokia Corporation about the purchase of their investment in Nokian tyres of Finland, I was accompanied by two Japanese colleagues from the European office. The meeting was organised with two executives from Nokia in a meeting room at Copenhagen airport. We took our positions on one side of the table. I was seated in the centre and the two Japanese colleagues were on either side of me. Once we introduced ourselves, neither of my Japanese colleagues spoke again. They made a few notes throughout the meeting, and by their silence it was clear that they were complicit with the position I was presenting. The discussion lasted about one and a half hours, and finally they found their voices when it was time to say goodbye. The meeting was successful and subsequent negotiations, which I also headed up, led to an agreement. The role of my colleagues was to intercede if I made a mistake, which fortunately did not happen, and to report accurately to higher levels of Japanese management. This way of working feels nothing like the team work one has come to expect in a western company.

English was the official language for internal meetings. Presentations at meetings were supported by slides which were in English as were the discussions that followed. Local employees could only join the company if their English was sufficiently good, yet Japanese staff that joined the teams seldom had similar levels of competency in English and so were not often engaged in the discussions. In my early years with the company, I was often upset when towards the end of a meeting the Japanese members would begin to converse in Japanese. I was never sure whether it was because they wanted to share what they had understood or if it was an attempt to prevent the Europeans from understanding what they were discussing. In hindsight, I think it was both.

When Europeans discussed in English or even in French, there were always a few Japanese who understood enough to decipher what was being discussed and who could, therefore, communicate these thoughts to their compatriots. On one occasion when discussion on a very important topic switched to Japanese, I addressed another Irish colleague in Gaelic and he responded in Gaelic. Some of the Japanese asked what language we were speaking. Their expressions changed when they realised it was a language that none of them understood. My intention had been to show them how it felt to be suddenly excluded from a discussion by switching language. However, my action was not appreciated. The Japanese felt perfectly entitled to exclude the locals whenever it suited them, but for Europeans to do the same was just not acceptable.

Trust and Prejudice

The issue of trust or the lack of trust is probably the most significant barrier to European / Japanese relations. Japanese corporations have been very successful in penetrating the European market with quality goods. The Japanese auto industry is one example. European exporters, on the other hand, have failed to make any significant impact in Japan.

Some of the biggest retailers in the world, including Carrefour, the French hypermarket chain, have invested heavily to open up in Japan only to close down and withdraw within less than a year. At the same time, Japanese consumers are huge consumers of quality brands from around the world; in fact they are the most passionate consumers I have seen anywhere in the world. Prestigious brands are statements of wealth and success. Many, such as Barbour, Rolex, Mont Blanc are European and are very sought-after in Japan. I believe that this paradox can be explained if we understand that while individual Japanese consumers prefer premium brands, corporate Japan is innately against foreign imports and Japanese society is still overcoming its history of isolation. Even today, more than 95% of people living in Japan are Japanese.

In 1633, shogun Lemitsu forbade travelling abroad and almost completely isolated Japan in 1639 by reducing the contacts to the outside world to very limited trade relations with China and the Netherlands in the port of Nagasaki. In addition, all foreign books were banned. [6]

---

[6] http://www.japan-guide.com/e/e2128

It was only during the second half of the 19th century, when the power of the Emperor Meiji was restored and with huge external pressure, that international trade was re-established, but the strong inherent national identity is still very strong today, and is protected. Japanese people who live abroad for more than six months are no longer eligible to give blood on their return to Japan. There may be some theoretical medical justification for this, but it is nevertheless consistent with a level of xenophobia that is not commonly encountered in Europe.

When we consider how the European nations evolved over many hundreds of years, we understand how Europe has become a mixture of cultures. The USA has been built on a steady influx of different ethnicities that has been going on for over two hundred years. Japan has remained an island nation with its language and culture largely protected by laws and codes that maintain its insularity. It is only by recognising this that we can begin to understand why many Japanese have a prejudice against non-Japanese cultures and values, and how this is reflected in their approach to business.

Many Japanese managers understand that these differences exist and that they are a barrier to business development. They have tried to adopt western methods at least on the surface, but you do not have to scratch very deeply to find the reality underneath.

For example, with very few exceptions, my experience was that women did not feature highly in Japanese management circles. During my fifteen years in the European headquarters only one female made it to the level of general manager. None made it beyond that level, and even the one that did had her contract terminated soon afterwards.

In the Japan headquarters, there were no females in high-level management positions for very many years. The top management recognised that their structure was conspicuous by its lack of women, so they appointed two women vice presidents and, in due course, appointed one non-executive female director to the board. These appointments were tokens whose aim was to give the impression that the company was modernising and incorporating respect for gender diversity in the workplace. The reality, however, was that it created internal problems. The male staff members of a female boss were uncomfortable working with and for a woman and were often openly critical of her. The place of women in Japanese society is clearly lower than that of the men, so having to work for a female boss creates great problems for many Japanese men. This was a fascinating contradiction to what I already described as the blind loyalty of the Japanese towards their boss.

I witnessed and experienced similar prejudice among Japanese staff when they worked in Europe. They were much more comfortable if they could report directly to a Japanese male boss. When they were in a position reporting to a European boss, they maximised their lateral contact with other Japanese and always appeared to have a role of reporting back to Japan headquarters. This dual reporting line allowed them to feel that they were not really reporting to a European and this behaviour was even nurtured by the top Japanese management. I watched European vice presidents with a Japanese boss above them and several Japanese reports below them, find themselves out of the loop as the people above and below discussed issues together and then presented them to the European vice president as a *fait accompli*.

The Japanese managers tend to believe that Japanese management practices are culture-unique and that no foreigners will ever fully understand the proper Japanese way of doing business. Because almost all of them have little or no experience working with non-Japanese colleagues or subordinates before, they often lack cross-cultural communication skills and are at a loss as to what to do, especially when they have to supervise Westerners. At the same time, they are afraid of being identified by their colleagues in Japan as *gaikoku boke* (foreign country fool) or *gaijin kabure* (quasi foreigner)- that is someone who has acquired the bad habits of a "peculiar" foreign country. They feel the strong need to stay "Japanese" even if they think that they should adopt or adapt to the proper ways of doing things in a foreign cultural environment. They also realise that their career advancement is more often tied to how they are viewed and evaluated by the superiors and colleagues at the home office than to good performance at the overseas posts. This psychological ambivalence causes the development of *kishikake konjo* or "temporary-stay mentality" that is not only counterproductive but also detrimental to maintaining good morale among the locally hired staff. [7]

The procession of CEOs that came through Bridgestone Europe recognised that the problem I have described was real. Several of them announced their intention to put European executives into key positions. These announcements invariably increased the motivation and the expectations of the Europeans, yet the top positions were unfailingly filled by Japanese executives. A few token positions were offered to Europeans but these were usually executives who had earned the reputation of blindly following orders. As such, they posed no threat and so inspired a certain kind of trust. Competence and suitability for the job were secondary criteria. And this was true even for those highly competent Europeans who showed true potential.

Trust and Confidence

Repeatedly, business opportunities were lost due to the length of time taken to analyse and present to top management. Opportunities to acquire businesses that would fit company strategy were missed because while the team was studying, evaluating, and re-analysing, our competitors would complete their study and buy the business. The key difference was that Japanese management was afraid of trusting what they were told by their non-Japanese staff. They had to study everything that was presented to them using their own limited Japanese resources. Even long serving loyal non-Japanese team members could not be trusted.

During 2010, I attended a high level round table discussion between representatives of the institutions of the European Union and a Japanese government delegation. During the opening speeches, several references to European / Japanese relations were made. The Copenhagen Climate Change conference had recently ended and the world realised that there was a new world order of power. Europe and Japan had been marginalised; the real discussions were between China and USA. At a subsequent EU-Japan roundtable, it was suggested that an opportunity for Europe and Japan to co-operate with each other had been created and that together they could have a stronger voice in the discussions about climate change and other global issues. Throughout the discussion, closer ties between the two regions were

---

[7] Doing Business with Japan, 2000, Kazuo Namiki, page 164.

encouraged although some of the speakers highlighted difficulties they had had when doing business in Japan and which would need to be overcome.

One of the last speakers at the discussion was the Director General of Trade in the European Commission. He had lived in Tokyo for 4 years while working for the European Union. He suggested that both sides should think more about the vision of what they want to achieve together before setting up working groups to study specific projects. He further expressed his view that the issue of mutual trust between Japan and Europe was a real problem and a barrier to development. For me, the very mention of distrust at such a high level meeting was a confirmation of what I had witnessed working inside a Japanese company.

Trust is not something the Japanese, or anyone for that matter, can suddenly develop. Trust has to be earned, and I have personal experience of working with a CEO for more than a year before earning any level of trust. But some Japanese executives came to Europe already conditioned to distrust local staff. Any European joining a Japanese company needs to be prepared to encounter this unfortunate attitude. The principle of *genbutsu genba*, which Bridgestone defines as "decision making based on verified, on site observation" basically means "don't believe anything you are told, and find out first hand by yourself"

Toyota has fourteen management principles called, "The Toyota Way", one of which is " *genchi* genbutsu" which has a very similar meaning to the Bridgestone principle, and is defined by Toyota as "go and see for yourself to thoroughly understand the situation". While I do understand and agree with these principles to a point, I believe that it can lead to micro managing and a situation where nothing is delegated and managers get sucked into such deep detail that they cannot maintain a helicopter view.

Paralysis by Analysis

It was common, in my experience, for the Japanese to avoid reporting upwards on some issues because they felt they had not analysed the issue deeply enough. In their mind, to report an issue without being able to answer all possible questions from their superiors was worse than not informing their superior at all.

As the company representative at an industry association, I received regular updates about political developments that could affect our business. I believed it was important to share this information with all my colleagues involved in standards and regulations worldwide. Consequently, I set up my email box to automatically forward these mails to a relevant list of people around the globe.

One Japanese colleague, Mike Ishimoto, based in Rome was on this circulation list. Mike was a technical genius. He understood technical details better than anyone I have ever met, and was one of the rare people who could explain engineering issues in English in a way that even non engineers could understand. However, his passion for detailed understanding made him impatient with the steady stream of brief reports that I was forwarding. As soon as he read one of the updates, which were intended as short executive summaries, he asked a series of questions designed to understand the issue more thoroughly. To be able to reply to his questions with the level of detail he wanted required that a staff member painstakingly research all contiguous information over several weeks. It was a resource we just did not have and whose efforts would be wasted because by the time the information was available, its benefits would have been lost.

Mike was so uncomfortable with unanalysed information being disseminated to counterparts in Japan, that he requested that either we do the research and prepare a detailed report on each issue or stop sending them. I argued that we should continue to send the information and then, if requested, to analyse selected parts more deeply, but Mike would not hear of it. His approach was so ingrained in his psyche that he preferred no report to a summary report. We stopped sending the emails but, as a result, key people in Japan were no longer aware in a timely basis of latest developments in the field.

Any one of the idiosyncrasies discussed above, when dealt with separately, could be handled by European staff, but when they all had to be managed at the same time, it became an almost insurmountable challenge for the European staff member. It is not surprising, therefore, to see the high level of staff turnover that Bridgestone had, and continues to have, in its European headquarters.

Chapter 3

Loyalty

Loyalty

I found the concept of loyalty amongst the Japanese to be very interesting. Loyalty to the company and loyalty to a boss are not necessarily complementary. I always felt a strong loyalty to the company and sometimes loyalty to individual bosses. However, my loyalty could be tested, particularly on occasions when my Japanese boss set directions which I believed were going to damage the company. Around me, I watched as my Japanese colleagues blindly followed the direction of the boss. For them there was no conflict: their attitude was, "If this is what the boss wants, I accept; that is what I will give him. He is my superior". The codes of behaviour related to the hierarchical structure among Japanese govern their decisions. Europeans are not conditioned to these codes, and consequently conflicts arise. I have known many Europeans who could not accept the notion that their opinion would not be considered, and that all that was required of them was their blind obedience. As a vice president, I believed that it was my duty to advise and even challenge the CEO's ideas, but all too often I found that final decisions had been made without proper consideration of facts that I had, or could have provided. I must emphasise here that this was not the case with all Japanese bosses, but it was absolutely true with a great many of them.

Learning Close to the Centre

On my first visit to Japan in 1990, I was part of an international group of trainees who spent two weeks on a company training course which consisted of technical and cultural coaching. The latter covered both Japanese and Bridgestone cultures. The group, which was exclusively male, came from countries as varied as the Ivory Coast, Iran, Algeria, Italy, the Netherlands, Greece, Turkey, United States, United Kingdom, Canada, and Spain and, in my case, Ireland.

At that time, the situation was as follows: Bridgestone was making efforts to extend its global reach. Business in the Americas was overtaking domestic business in Japan, and other parts of the world, including Europe, were growing in importance. As a part of this internationalisation, a few non-Japanese staff members had joined the line-up in the Tokyo head office. They were involved in organising and delivering training courses for overseas team members.

Regrettably, a change of global leadership took place soon after 1990, and the global training programme was cancelled as a cost-saving strategy. The result was that the non-Japanese who left Bridgestone were not replaced. The new CEO did not believe that non-Japanese were needed in the head office nor did he consider the training of international staff in the ways of the Japanese to be of any importance.

I say that the decision was regrettable because, as one of the last of the international trainees to have taken part in the programme, I believe that I gained insights and understandings of the Japanese without which I could never have lasted in the company for another twenty-two years. During the two weeks of intensive training in Tokyo, all the participants were impressed by the force of the dedication to the company that we witnessed amongst employees. We also felt our own commitment and engagement intensifying. It was as if we were learning a new religion.

Towards the end of the second week, we were asked to prepare for a farewell party, a ceremonial affair to be attended by people from several departments in the head office, as well as all the trainees. During the evening, our test results were announced and certificates were awarded. At the end of the evening, everyone joined in singing the company song, first in Japanese, and then in English. The theme of the song was *pride* - how proud we were to work for the great Bridgestone Company.

I subsequently learned that all the large Japanese corporations have company songs. Their purpose was not unlike that which spurred communist societies to encourage school children to sing songs that glorified their leader: encourage engagement, inspire loyalty, and nurture deep, emotional bonds.

I returned to Ireland committed to building the newly-established

Bridgestone Ireland into a leader in the industry. Using methods more appropriate to a western company, I fostered commitment, dedication and loyalty among the employees. It was clear that it would be impossible to emulate the same values and engagement of Japanese employees, but a high level of commitment could still be nurtured. One of the keys to this was to show my own commitment and belief in the company and to lead by example.

Unfortunately, during my subsequent years in Brussels, I never witnessed the same effort from top management to cultivate the engagement of employees, and I am convinced that this was one of the major failings of the company after 1990. If the European employees had been coached, mentored and led by example, their effort and commitment would have been far greater. Instead, the Japanese management in Europe fostered a two-level company. The first level was reserved for the Japanese members stationed in Europe who enjoyed most of the senior positions; the second level European employees, who like me and two hundred other staff, were relegated to a *de facto* outsider role.

Full Commitment

During the inter-cultural training period, one of the major cultural differences that impressed me was the dedication of the Japanese employees to their company. We got to know some of the local members of the training team and learned from them that the most important day in their lives was the day they were accepted into the Bridgestone Corporation. Many of them had degrees from the best universities in Japan and were among thousands of graduates who had applied to the top companies in Japan. After a rigorous interview and selection process, those selected entered the company to begin what would become a lifetime career path.

I never learned what the pay level was for the new recruits, but I do know that they were provided with sleeping accommodation in company dormitories and were bound by very strict rules and curfews. Older employees, who were more established in the company, lived in apartments further away from the city centre. They described their working commute as a daily ritual, "I leave my apartment at 06:30 in the morning to catch the train at 06:50. The train is always full, so usually I have to stand for the ninety minutes until I arrive at Tokyo station. I leave the office at around 21:00 and take the 21:30 train back home. My wife will have a meal waiting for me at 11:30 before I go to bed."

I remember one engineer, Tashiro, telling me that he had to work on Saturdays to keep on top of the paperwork but then he would leave the office in the early afternoon so that he could see his children before they went to bed. They would enjoy Sundays together knowing that he would not see them again until the following Saturday afternoon. Tashiro and others like him were not complaining; they were telling us what it was like to work for the company. The European and American trainees could not imagine living in this way, but for the Japanese to have a job for life in one of the major Japanese corporations was regarded as a proof of success. It offered a status and fulfilment for which they, in return, would dedicate themselves to the company above all else.

Following the famous North American product recall crisis in 2000, the Japanese employees stationed in Europe were called to a meeting in Brussels where the company's survival strategy was explained to them. This measure was intended as an affirmation of faith in the company and a promise that their future was secure as long as the employees continued to work hard. No such meeting was held for the European employees. At this time of crisis, when we were working twelve to fourteen hours a day on crisis management in addition to the normal work, no-one took the time to ensure that the European employees maintained their faith and commitment. The gap between the two groups of employees widened as a result.

When respect for diversity was introduced as a stated objective of the company's CSR list, I thought back to that time of crisis. It is sensible to strive for a gender and age balance in the management of the company, just as it is enlightened to employ many different nationalities, but, for all their rhetoric and stated objectives, Japanese companies were never more insular than when crisis hit. At these times, they would withdraw into their own national group, closet themselves in secret, and no longer openly discuss business matters with their western colleagues. When I discussed this phenomenon with close Japanese colleagues, they were sympathetic to my concern but would inevitably explain that the Japanese close network was simply a tighter and more important one.

Independent Thinking – Follow the Examples

My invitation to join the European headquarters of Bridgestone came as a result of my successful development of the Irish subsidiary in the first 7 years after its foundation. I had increased the business and market share, built a great team, kept operating costs low and beat the forecasted budget every year. The most valuable tool I had throughout those eventful years was my autonomy. Once the annual budget was set, I was free to control prices, develop distribution channels and implement marketing programs. If a decision needed to be taken, I could take it. As long as I delivered the budgeted results in sales, profit and market share, everything else was left to me.

One of the early shocks I had after moving to the European headquarters was the discovery that I had forfeited my decision-making power. Initially, I was responsible for sales to the major manufacturers of trucks and agricultural tractors. Every deal or proposal had to be approved by a higher authority, and the process of discussing how and why we had arrived at a proposal required endless discussion and necessitated exhaustive data and graphs. I was often reminded of a former colleague's dictum that, "a graph a day keeps the Japanese away".

Integrating into the new environment was a real challenge. I was enthusiastic, energetic, and ready to make an impact, but I received little or no directions about how I was supposed to work. Some years later I read Kevin Bucknall's insights about working for a Japanese company.

"What the heck am I supposed to do?" You will rarely have a job description or anyone to explain how to do the job you have been given. Learning in Japan is traditionally done by watching, listening and imitating, rather than by someone delivering a structured outline of a discipline. This applies in business, as well as in areas as diverse as flower arranging and pottery making. Zen Buddhism eschews formal teaching as well as the use of logic, and its influence is powerful.

Sitting around with little to do can be frustrating and you will probably feel much of your time is being wasted or your abilities underused. There is not much you can do about it and making waves by complaining will not endear you to your boss or group. You are expected to watch and learn as you go, and at the same time listen to and pick up advice, which itself will be low key and perhaps shyly offered. It would be exceptional to be put through a formal training programme. Many Japanese learn the ropes by observation and practical on-the-job experience over a period of years.

What can make it more difficult for you is that it is bad manners to ask direct questions of your superior, so that if you are working in a Japanese company and do not know what you should be doing, your normal response (to ask your boss) is not available." [8]

It would have helped me and others had we read his book before coming to Brussels. As my focus shifted increasingly to understanding how to behave, my enthusiasm and energy diminished. All the big ideas I had brought to Brussels were stored away or forgotten, and my pace adapted to the new environment. In my new world, my role was reduced to seeding ideas and supporting them with endless analysis.

Loss of Face

Employees who exhibit deep loyalty to the company are often protected from loss of face when things go wrong. Commitment is rewarded with job security. Consequently, the Japanese employees make huge personal sacrifices in their "patriotism" towards the company, and they are prepared to suffer for its greater good. One sacrifice, however, is unthinkable, that is, loss of face.

Perhaps it comes from the ancient Chinese belief:

Loss of money = nothing lost.
Loss of Health = much lost.
Loss of honour = everything lost.

In their efforts to protect an employee from losing face, a range of tactics and processes are used. A CEO that I have mentioned already

---

[8] Japan: Doing Business in a Unique Culture. 2006, Kevin B. Bucknall,p.179.

was suddenly called back to Japan because the business in Europe was collapsing under his mismanagement. The announcement of his departure explained that his expertise was urgently needed at the head office and that he would return as a "special advisor" to the group chairman. In preparation for the farewell dinner for the "special advisor", I was asked to write a speech. I was instructed to include a list of his achievements during his short time in Europe. The only way I could do this was to catalogue major events that had occurred during his tenure and to suggest that they were his personal achievements. These included establishing a new factory and expanding the research and development facilities. The speech was a great success. The departing CEO stood up and remarked that until that very moment he had not actually understood how much he had achieved. My mission was accomplished. He left Europe without the shame of his mismanagement becoming public. The reality was that all the projects that I had listed had all been planned and started before his arrival in Europe.

Unaji, who left his indelible mark everywhere he went, was retired from the company at the age of 58. It was not his wish to do so. He tried very hard to find employment elsewhere but because of his reputation, which reached far beyond the company itself, he was unsuccessful. Yet, any mention of his departure from the company was met with protests that he had chosen to retire after long and dedicated service to the company. Once again, the same consideration did not apply to the non-Japanese. Unaji, who took pleasure in reducing grown men to tears and publicly humiliating them, was protected. European managers who no longer met the requirements of their positions were unceremoniously dismissed, and only rarely reassigned to new positions as their Japanese counterparts would have been. These differences in treatment only became clear to me after several years of service and following frequent changes in top management. While I was on my induction training in Japan, none of these traits were obvious. I made the mistake of believing that as I immersed myself in the company culture and conformed to its practices, I was being welcomed with the same enthusiasm as any Japanese recruit and that I would be treated according to the same rules.

Hierarchy

One thing that was made clear from the beginning of my employment, however, was the importance of the hierarchical structure of Japanese companies. Westerners were used to showing respect for superiors, but they expected to be treated with consideration in return. One day, during our training, we were summoned to the board room to "meet" some of the top management. A parade of senior executives entered and took up their positions at one end of the table. We were expected to gaze at them in awe. For the Japanese in our group, actually being in the same room with these godlike men was one of the highlights of the week. For us, there was a mixture of feelings: we were curious about the attitude of the junior Japanese towards their superiors, but we regretted the realisation that an invisible barrier existed between us and them.

Years later in Europe, I accompanied the European CEO, Shinagawa to a dinner which our company was sponsoring. I introduced him to several ambassadors and high-ranking officials from the European Commission. He went through the usual Japanese protocol of respectfully exchanging business cards with each of them, and they, in turn, showed the respect due to his position. The following day, I met Shinagawa's secretary who was busy photocopying the collected business cards on to two pages to be faxed to Tokyo to show the number of high-level people he had met at the dinner. I learned that mixing and meeting with prominent people is very important to the Japanese; I had yet to learn that there are clear hierarchies and one must learn one's place in them quickly.

I witnessed several examples, some of them very funny, of junior Japanese trainees making supreme efforts to avoid disturbing their superior unnecessarily. One day, the serving CEO in Europe, Mizutani, was making a presentation of a report to a group of managers. He had called on a junior Japanese trainee, Ishii, to set up his projector on the table behind him while he continued to speak to us. When Ishii had completed his task, he looked around to see how we could return to his seat without disturbing Mizutani whose back was turned to him. Ishii decided that he could not walk in front of Mizutani and proceeded to consider the alternatives. These included using the door that led out of the room, but opening the door and leaving would be disrespectful as well as disruptive. He then noticed that the table on which the PC and projector sat had four very thin legs. He realised that there was enough room for his thin body to climb through and reach his seat on the other side of the room. Ishii's every thought was clear to all of us looking on. Finally, he made his decision. He went down on the floor and began to sidle through. By this time the audience, most of who were chuckling, was riveted on his movements and had completely lost interest in the CEO's presentation. Here was our chairman and CEO delivering an important message to his management team and behind him a young Japanese trainee was on his hands and knees climbing between the legs of a table. Mizutani turned to see what was going on, and almost simultaneously Ishii's foot hit one of the legs of the table. The projector tilted and, with it, the slide that was being projected. Mizutani, now clearly irritated, shouted at Ishii, "What are you doing?" Ishii automatically jumped up. As he did so, he banged his head on the table and sent the projector off balance yet again. By this point, the audience released the full force of its laughter. Ishii emerged from under the table with the weight of his shame bearing down on him. He did not dare meet the gaze of Mizutani. Instead, he bowed energetically and apologised profusely and then continued to bow and apologise as he slunk towards his seat. For the audience it had been like watching a comedy sketch. For Ishii, it was the price he paid for not wanting to disturb his superior.

Interaction between Non-Japanese and Their Japanese Superiors.

When I moved to the European headquarters in 1997, there was no induction process. I relied on what I had learned on my training course in Japan 7 years before. Having a manager in the same building was a return to the way I had worked in the days before Bridgestone. Although I missed the autonomy of being in charge of a company, I welcomed the idea of being able to discuss important topics with my superior. I always believed in the open door policy, and had practiced it myself. I soon learned that my new boss, Yasuka, did not operate the same way.

Any time I tried to speak with him, he made it clear that he had no time and never proposed a more suitable one. I began to build relationships with immediate colleagues and learned what I needed to learn from them. After a month, I began to feel uncomfortable with the reporting structure. I had not yet had a meeting with Yasuka who had, after all, been instrumental in convincing me to come to Brussels. I had received no briefing, no explanation of objectives, and no guidelines or direction. I wondered if I had done something wrong. Then, one evening, I saw Yasuka approaching my desk. I had no idea what he might want, but hoped that he might take the opportunity to ask how I was getting on and discuss the current priority issues. He asked if I was scheduled to travel anywhere that week. I assumed he was going to ask me to travel, perhaps even accompany him on a business trip. I replied that I could change my arrangements but Yasuka seemed only interested in knowing my travel plans and especially when I would be returning to Brussels if travel was planned. When I told him about a day trip to visit Renault in Lyon, his face relaxed. "Oh good," he exclaimed. "Could you please pick up 200 Mild Seven cigarettes from the duty free on your way". I was stunned. I had waited for a month for my first conversation with my new boss, and when it came it was to ask me to run an errand for him. When I assured him that I would have his cigarettes for him by Friday, he thanked me and withdrew. With few exceptions, life in the corporate headquarters continued in this vein. It became necessary to set a meeting to set a meeting.

The European CEO at that time was Imai-san, an accountant by training who was nearing retirement. In my years as managing director of Bridgestone Ireland, I had met Imai in Brussels, and he had visited Ireland several times. As he was an 8 handicap golfer, I had arranged a golf game for him on one of Ireland's most prestigious courses on the Saturday following a Friday board meeting. He was pleased by the offer, and invited me to enjoy dinner with him and other executives. We spent several hours together on the Friday evening. I had learned that time spent in the company of others on a golf course could break down barriers and forge friendships that might become very useful. I believed that a day of shared golf and an evening of talk and dinner had brought our relationship to a new level. I had expected to build on this relationship when I moved to Brussels, but was disappointed to find that the dynamics were very different in the head office. Now, instead of being the main contact in a subsidiary company, I was one of more than a hundred employees. Imai tended to stay in his office and delegate to his direct reports. He almost never interacted with the European staff members, and there was a huge separation between him and the locals.

Work Ethic – Working Hours – Single Mindedness

Accepting a business-sponsored invitation to golf on a weekday was out of the question for managers and employees in a Japanese company. I had come from Ireland where I often received more than ten invitations each summer. In Belgium, corporate golf was less common; even taking a day of vacation was frowned upon and considered as proof of lack of commitment to the company. This notion that not taking vacation time or working very long hours was a necessary sacrifice was something that Unaji tried to instill in his European staff. He believed that he could get the Europeans to think and act like Japanese. As for accepting an invitation to play golf during the working week, this would always be viewed as a statement of disloyalty.

I never saw a Japanese colleague accept a golf invitation on a weekday. Conversely, I almost never saw a Japanese colleague decline a golf invitation on a weekend. Japanese golfers are passionate about golf. What surprised me was that the same men, who worked until 9 o'clock every evening even while their wives and children were home alone, would play golf all day on Saturday or Sunday or even both. The attitude to work / life balance is distinctly different between Japanese and European managers and staff. If Japanese companies are to succeed in Europe they need to understand, observe and encourage a more balanced approach to work. For Europeans considering a job with a Japanese corporation, they should keep in mind that even though the official working hours are 35 or 37.5 or 40 hours per week, they need to be prepared to work 50 hours or more, and that actually taking full holiday entitlements will raise eyebrows and doubts about commitment.

Blind Obedience

There is also an unwritten law that if a Japanese boss sets a direction or policy, then it cannot be wrong. Even if it is patently wrong, it is right. Junior Japanese will follow the stated direction regardless of whether it is good for the company or not. I found this approach to be completely at odds with the European way of thinking. Responsible European managers would naturally challenge a hypothesis or a proposal from their superior in order to make sure that it was the best idea. They would want to share their informed opinion. For some Japanese management this process of decision making was completely unacceptable. The idea that a European manager would challenge his boss's idea was considered insulting, disloyal, and uncooperative.

Never Mind the Reality – Gather Data that Looks Like Facts

At one point I worked with a Japanese director, Tenshi, who reported to me. One of his tasks was to organise a consumer and trade research project. This was a big investment because it was undertaken by a professional research company. The objective was to measure the effectiveness of the company's sponsorship of Formula 1.

Tenshi was difficult to manage. He had been transferred from the United States where he had been a specialist on retail operations. His assignment in Europe was not meeting his ambitions, and he believed that he was destined for far more important positions. It particularly irked him that I had come from a small market, Ireland, and yet had risen to the position of vice president. He repeatedly bypassed me to discuss matters with more senior Japanese managers; interacting with executives at a level which he felt befitted his own perception of his true status, fed his hurt ego, and assuaged his battered self-image.

While he focused on the research project, he worked long and hard with the research company to identify the target groups and to define the questions to be asked during face to face interviews. I had delegated the preparation work to him but insisted that I wanted a full review of the project before we moved forward. Tenshi tried to avoid the review, arguing that it would be impossible to meet our deadlines if any changes were required at this late stage. I insisted and persisted.

As I reviewed the questions, I noted a very strong bias towards Formula 1 fans. For example, instead of asking if the interviewee actually liked to watch Formula 1 racing, questions only measured how often they watched. When I pointed this out to Tenshi and suggested that we would not get a true picture of what we needed to know from these questions, he grew very angry. Because I knew how much was being invested in the research, I was determined to get it right. As our argument continued, he began coaching me in the purpose of research and pointed out that his expert experience had taught him that its main objective was to gather data that would confirm the chosen direction. In other words, the result of our research should validate the positive effect of our involvement in Formula 1 on consumers and business partners. In Tenshi's opinion, what we did not want were findings that put into question our involvement in Formula 1. I was shocked.

Tenshi was adamant that he would not change his position and sought support from my boss, the infamous Unaji. Unsurprisingly, Unaji who loved to attend Formula 1 events, backed Tenshi, and I was forced to withdraw my objections. As my arguments were dismissed one after the other, I concluded that the most striking characteristics of Japanese attitudes to working with Europeans were at work: a Japanese colleague owes blind loyalty to a Japanese boss; he owes no such thing to a non-Japanese boss.

Experiences like this one, of which there were many, led to me re-evaluate my role. There were many examples to attest to the fact that my authority and position were respected, but I nevertheless had understood that I could, at any time, be undermined by junior Japanese colleagues. That a European manager could be rendered powerless by the mechanisms that excluded them from the central decision-making processes was very reassuring for many Japanese. Yet, it was these very processes and mechanisms that undermined the confidence of the Europeans who were regularly confronted with their vulnerability in a system such as this one.

Chapter 4

Xenophobia

Cultural differences- understanding Europe- Ethics-Superiority

Cultural differences exist at several levels. There are differences in habits and behaviour between Northern Europeans and Southern Europeans for example. But greater differences become apparent between nationalities with very different origins. We know that there is not one generic European culture and Europeans have to deal with the differences among themselves on a daily basis. The Brussels Institutions are often described as offices of compromise but they do work.

The cultural differences between Japanese and Europeans are much deeper than those among Europeans. Dealing with these differences is complicated, especially in the workplace

In her book, *Fear and Trembling*, Amélie Nothomb talks about one of her favourite films from her youth, *Merry Christmas Mr. Lawrence*, which is set in a war-time prisoner of war camp in the Pacific. Nothomb believes that the film could be viewed as a metaphor for relations among people. "Behind the surface conflict lies reciprocated curiosity. Misunderstandings hide a genuine desire to understand one another".[9]

While I agree that she touches on a truth, I believe that she underestimates the force of prejudice and xenophobia in the conflicts and misunderstandings that occur between human beings. In order that people understand one another, they need to recognise their differences and accept them. In business environments this can be complicated to achieve, and more needs to be done in soft skills training for both managers and staff.

---

[9] Fear and Trembling. Amélie Nothomb. 1999. page 110

Many of the differences can be understood by people with an open mind and a desire to know other cultures. But what are the roots of these differences in attitudes?

Historical Development

I suggest that the starting point is an historical one. Japan is an ancient civilization that has existed for centuries on a small group of islands which have been spared "contamination" from other cultures. Japanese history traces its origins back as far as the JŌMON period, that is, 14000 BC. The current Imperial family has reigned since about 700 AD. Records show that waves of Japanese emigrated to Pacific countries and to the west coast of America during the twentieth century, but there is little evidence of them returning to Japan. During the Tokugawa period (1600 – 1868)Christians and foreigners were almost completely banned from entering Japan. The end of this period marked the beginning of the period of growth of Japan as an economic power. The eighteenth and nineteenth centuries were also the period of the foundation of the United States of America. Hundreds of thousands of Europeans from all over Europe moved to the east coast of America and gradually pushed across the country to the Pacific coast. Over the centuries, these immigrants mixed with the Mexicans, descendants of Africans and the indigenous Indians who were living there: America's population today is a result of this ebb and flow of diverse populations and exchange of cultures. While this was happening in Europe and America, Japan remained an insular nation whose society was comparatively untouched by outside influences. At the same time, the shape of Europe's borders changed many times and the cultures of Asians, Hispanics, North Africans and Slavs mixed irreversibly in both periods of peace and war.

Many elements of Japanese culture continued to be passed down unchanged through successive generations and today, for the Japanese, as scholar and former United States ambassador to Japan, Edwin O. Reischauer comments, "the line between the 'we' of the Japanese as a national group and the 'they' of the rest of mankind seems to be sharper for them. They appear to have a greater feeling of group solidarity and a correspondingly stronger sense of their difference from others." [10]

First Experiences

Early in my career, my exposure to Japanese people was limited to greeting visiting representatives. My colleagues and I were effectively customers and we were met and treated with deep respect. We were very impressed with the manners and graciousness of the Japanese people, and it was almost impossible to imagine that there was a darker side to their character. I would only make the discovery quite a few years later.

When Bridgestone agreed to a feasibility study of the market in Ireland with a view to setting up a subsidiary company, a junior analyst from Tokyo was sent to our offices in Dublin. Nishiyama was in his twenties, and for him, the opportunity to travel to a country in Europe was akin to winning a small lottery. It was agreed that he would spend five days with us analysing data to prepare his report, but because his visit coincided with Saint Patrick's Day when all Dublin offices were closed, his time with us was reduced to 4 days. As the person hosting him, I had to take care of him on the holiday as well as during the working days and evenings. As an inexperienced cross-cultural communicator at that time, it turned out to be a very stressful week for me. Nishiyama was only comfortable when he was sitting at a desk with piles of monthly reports and a calculator, and those working near him reported that they were sure that they had seen sparks flying from his calculator as he speedily accumulated endless rows of figures.

I quickly learned that Nishiyama did not speak English very well. He referred to his dictionary constantly, and just barely understood the topics we were discussing - certainly not much more. I was nevertheless determined to make his visit as pleasant as possible because, after all, we were hoping that he would write a favourable report, but the only thing I could find in common with Nishiyama was a shared love of food. He was a portly young man and wanted to taste as many different cuisines as he could during his European visit. He had no interest in visiting the one and only Japanese restaurant that existed in Dublin at that time, and preferred discovering anything that

---

[10] The Japan Project. The role of traditional attitudes in Modern Japan. 2003
The American Forum for Global education. www.globaled.org

could be considered as local cuisine or dishes that he was unlikely to encounter again in other countries. So much of our evenings were spent offering him restaurant food that he relished. Years later, I discovered that Nishiyama's attitude was not the norm: an open mind towards foreign tastes and customs was not common among the Japanese. Nishiyama's five -day visit was a challenging but overall enjoyable time because of his willingness to explore our Irish world. For me, it was an introduction to managing cultural differences that would become a lifetime's work.

As a Visitor in Japan

For the western tourist visiting Japan, the experience is unique. There are classic tourist destinations such as Tokyo Tower which is taller than the Eiffel Tower in Paris, but which is neither very beautiful nor well-known outside Japan; there are endless temples that are promoted as must-see destinations, and there are various parks and gardens. Then, of course, there are shopping areas with the enormous stores and the garish neon signs. Tourists are welcome and politely catered for at all these locations. Elsewhere, visitors encounter a very different reception. In many bars, clubs and local restaurants foreigners are not welcome because the "foreigner" disturbs the regular customers. As a guest of local businessmen, I enjoyed visits to some of these bars and clubs, and as the guest of a local man, my presence was tolerated. It was always made clear, however, that I was an outsider. The hosts were never rude, but neither were they friendly.

In 1999, I participated in hosting a group of visitors representing one of Bridgestone's biggest customers to the Tokyo headquarters. We visited manufacturing plants, a major research centre and the ancient city of Kyoto. The Tokyo-based hosts provided the highest level of hospitality imaginable. We dined in the finest restaurants, ate Kobe beef, toured celebrated sites and, on the final evening, visited a Geisha House. Later, many of my Japanese colleagues who did not participate in the visit expressed their envy. Like most Japanese, they could not afford to eat Kobe beef, and visiting a Geisha House was a rare privilege not only for the non-Japanese visitor but for most Japanese as well. It was an honour usually reserved for top Japanese businessmen.

On other visits to Japan I learned that the codes of hospitality are applied differently to visitors who are accompanied by Japanese hosts and those who are not. When I was accompanied only by westerners, entering bars and restaurants was no easy task. It was difficult for us to grasp the idea that many Japanese small businesses were more interested in keeping us out than taking our money.

I was accustomed to getting to know people in Europe through direct one-to-one conversation and I was alert to body language. In the West, facial expression is one means of communication; in Japan, looking at someone directly in the eyes or touching them is frowned upon. This creates an additional barrier for westerners when they want to get to know someone in Japan or if they want to be able to communicate comfortably with them.

An Island Nation

I am convinced that the xenophobia that exists among the Japanese derives from a long history of isolation and the simple fact that they are an island nation. I grew up in an island nation, albeit a much smaller one. I recall that during my childhood I rarely saw a person who was visibly different. The Irish just never saw many "foreigners" before the economic boom of the 1990s when Ireland began welcoming immigrants and tourists who, for the first time in its history, came in hundreds of thousands. Until then, over long centuries of economic hardship, the Irish had emigrated all over the world and had adapted wherever they had made their homes. The newcomers integrated comfortably into a society that proved to be hospitable towards them.

The difference between these two island nations is that Japan has a longer history and stricter codes governing it. The Irish character is more personable and empathetic. The Japanese believe in their superiority. This influences their business behaviour and fosters many of the problems that they face doing business in the West. I expect that other ancient Asian societies will manifest similar attitudes as they establish their corporate footholds in the west. I would encourage them to consider the experiences of those who have gone before them when they prepare their strategies. They must consider and accept local codes of behaviour and recognise that their hosts are not inferior, merely different.

Cultural Differences - Minor and Major.

Working in a pan-European environment implies cultural differences even among the different Europeans. The French greet everyone with a kiss in the morning; the Germans address each other formally and maintain a respectable distance from each other. I once asked a German colleague how long one would wait before calling someone by their first name. He replied that in the case of a woman you would probably wait until you were sleeping with her. Another colleague who thoroughly enjoyed the experience of living in a diverse multi-cultural environment once mused that, "the thing I love about living in Belgium is the mixture of customs one finds. If I go to dinner with friends in the East we eat cheese before dinner, if I am visiting friends in the West we eat cheese after dinner". He was referring to locations no more than thirty minutes east and west of Brussels. Imagine how much more complex it becomes to work and live if you add to this already complex pan-European reality, the additional layer of the idiosyncratic styles of Japanese management and colleagues.

Unaji comes to mind again. He had fixed ideas about everything, and when we add to this characteristic his legendary rudeness and lack of concern for anyone's feelings, we have a recipe for some of the most fascinating examples of cultural misunderstanding one could imagine. In the course of a global meeting which the European business unit was hosting in Rome, we had planned an afternoon break to give the visitors from overseas a tour of Rome. Delegates had come from the USA, Canada, Australia and Japan and had joined the European delegates of whom I was one. We assembled in downtown Rome at the Piazza Navona where our private tour bus and guide were waiting. Unaji was amongst the first to board the bus. He slid into the front seat which was normally reserved for the tour guide. The rest of the group took their seats. In due course, a young tour guide boarded. She smiled at Unaji and politely told him that he was sitting in her seat. He replied that he was there first. She was clearly surprised by his response but maintained her polite demeanour and respectfully explained that as she was the tour guide, she needed to sit in the seat closest to the microphone and to the driver. Unaji's temper flared and our hearts sank. He growled that it was his seat and that he was not moving. The argument continued until the tour guide told the driver that she was no longer willing to serve as the guide for the group, and promptly departed. The tour proceeded without her. One of our colleagues who had lived in Rome for a few years took the young lady's role and pointed out various buildings that he was able to identify. Unaji remained unperturbed in his seat.

At another pan-European meeting in Seville, the delegates had taken morning flights from all over Europe and arrived at the hotel in time to have a late lunch together. The gathering was hosted by our Spanish office. Everyone made a lunch choice from the menu, but Unaji who was last to order, declared, "I want paella". The waiter, who did not speak English, explained to one of our Spanish hosts that paella was neither on the menu nor a local dish in Seville. Our senior Spanish manager murmured this information to Unaji who barked "I'm in Spain am I not? I want paella." Negotiations ensued with the chef until he agreed to make paella but warned that it would take an additional forty-five minutes to prepare. Unaji grunted ungratefully, "I will have the paella". The other delegates, who were appalled by what they had witnessed, had to wait until the paella was served before they could eat their lunch. Unaji ignored all of them and ate his paella in silence.

Europe Versus the Countries of Europe

Successful businesses in Europe adapt to the tastes, preferences and habits of their customers. In its basic form, this means speaking to customers in their own language. For example, the Irish butter maker, Kerrygold makes butter with less salt for the Benelux market because it is the preference of the people in that particular market. Understanding the likes and dislikes of individual customer groups is the result of extensive learning and experience within the market.

Japanese executives with whom I worked had limited understanding of the complexities of the European market. Those who had spent time in North America and who were now working in Europe assumed that they would be in familiar territory in their new positions. For them, Americans and Europeans were "westerners" and therefore were identical. In Tokyo, they talked about the United States market and then they talked about the European market as if they were speaking about the same thing. The problem is that it is a very serious mistake to consider Europe as a single market for automotive products like tyres. It is no accident that the French market is dominated by French cars, the German market by German cars and the Italian market by Italian cars. The competitive environment and the channels of distribution can differ immensely from one European country to another and the smart marketer will adjust his strategy keeping these differences in mind.

While some of my Japanese colleagues grudgingly accepted that these differences existed, the major decision-makers believed they knew better. During most of my time in the European organization, it operated with a dedicated sales team in which each market tapped into local knowledge and worked in the local language. This was not appreciated either as a strength or as a necessity by the most senior Japanese managers.

In 1999, we held a pan-European incentive trip which brought together about 150 dealers and their wives from all over Europe for a visit to Japan to see the Bridgestone facilities and to enjoy a cultural tour. On the second evening, a gala dinner was organised in a grand ballroom where top management from the head office including the global CEO of the time, Kato, gathered. Although he did not speak English well, he delivered his welcome speech in English. Although it was clear to me that in fact, 70% of those present could not speak English, Kato had assumed that everyone in Europe could speak or understand English. This led to some rather difficult moments for me when one of Kato's assistants informed me that Kato wanted to make a tour of the room and meet all the dealers. There was no-one in the room who knew them all. Each had qualified to be there as a result of a sales contest that had nothing to do with the size of their dealership, but rather by the amount by which they had increased their purchases in the preceding six months. I was informed that I should make the introductions. As we approached each table, I had to identify the Bridgestone representative among the group, ask him to introduce Kato to his guests, and then in turn, present all the people at the table to Kato. Kato and his entourage did not quite understand why I was not speaking Finnish, Italian, Spanish, German and so on, or why none of the guests were able to respond to his poor English. At one point, when we introduced the dealer from Estonia, he openly wondered if we were not fabricating countries. Kato had assumed that we were a homogeneous group because we were Europeans. He had no idea about the geographic or cultural diversity that was present in the room.

Throughout the evening, he behaved according to Japanese protocol and this often made the guests uneasy. Nothing was more disconcerting for the guests than the moment Kato decided that the evening was over. He suddenly rose from his seat, went to the exit and stood there ready to bid goodnight to each individual as they left. It was clear that he had decided that it was time for everyone to leave. The guests, many of whom had consumed a good deal of alcohol, were not ready to go and were, in fact, just beginning to settle in for what they expected to be a very late night. There was a standoff. Kato insisted that he had to say good-bye to everyone because he should be the last to leave. However, the dealers had no intention of leaving and even offered to pay for their own drinks so that they could stay on. Finally, we convinced the dealers to thank Kato, say good-night and leave the room. We also told them that they could re-enter the room by another door. It was a ridiculous charade that revealed, above all, Kato's lack of even the slightest understanding of the cultural differences that were at play that evening.

In fact, the whole week in Japan highlighted the lack of intercultural understanding that reigned amongst the group. Examples fell like rain on the week. To begin with, several of the European dealers just could not adapt to the cultural context into which they had touched down. They admired the careful arrangements that the Japanese had made, but they were not ready to play by the rules. For example, every day the buses arrived and departed on schedule; every day the Irish and the Italians in the group were late. The Germans were always the first on the bus and the Italians were always the last. The Germans were invariably annoyed and the Italians unfailingly bewildered by the angry stares that greeted them when they arrived fifteen minutes late every day. On another evening, a western style barbeque was planned at a brewery. When we arrived, the Spanish were thrilled to find baskets of bread on every table; they cheered because they had not seen bread for several days and were missing it. It was only minutes before they got down to the business of breaking what, for them, had been a fast. As for the French, when they discovered the selection of cheeses that was set out, they devoured what they could eat even before they went anywhere near the barbecue. During a tour of Kyoto, the group stopped for lunch at a classic Japanese restaurant. An Irish woman literally broke into tears after a third bowl of unrecognizable food was placed before her. Unwilling to try anything on her plate, she boldly asked if she could be served a simple ham sandwich.

These are all examples of culture shock common among people who have not travelled or who have never experienced different cultures. If a company wants to establish itself globally and gain a degree of respectability in a foreign country, then it must take responsibility for the intercultural education of its employees. As well, it should expect that cultural exchange can be transformational for the company itself. Corporations operating globally must abandon the idea that change is dangerous because it invariably dilutes the founding values of the company. Differences must be embraced. In my experience, it became clear that Bridgestone does not do this very well nor does it appear to understand that it is a challenge that will sooner or later need to be tackled.

The View of Europe

Japanese and other Asian managers who want to build a winning strategy for the European market cannot disregard the diversity of languages and cultures that exist in Europe. They must broaden their thinking and revise their assumptions that because they view Europeans and Americans as "westerners", they are basically the same as each other. Companies that take the high level view that Europe is one market of 400 million people, will not be as successful as a company that tailors its offers to the market conditions that vary across the continent.

If one is viewing the world from the top floor of a Tokyo office building, it is easy to see Europe as a single market. After all, the top executives sitting in these comfortable offices are reading financial and political journals that talk about the single European market. Indeed the European Commission is constantly regulating standards and rules that make it legally impossible not to deal with the European market as a single entity. This is all good news for the company that wants to sell its products in European countries. However, this convenience does not consider the cultures, habits and preferences of individual consumers in each country. Consumers will continue to exercise their right to make their own choice from what is available on the market, so companies that can adapt to the preferences of different customer groups will be the winners. Therefore, a company that really wants to succeed in Europe will have to research and tailor its products, or at least the way their products are sold, to each European market. Furthermore, they will have to adjust their communication to the different audiences.

Local companies that tailor their channels of distribution to meet the needs of the local market have a distinct advantage. The Japanese simply do not understand this. They believe that what works in Japan should work in Europe and that what works in one European country should work in another. They are wrong.

No one can deny that Japanese companies provide world class products and manufacturing processes. They may be leaders in developing good products, but they have a long way to go before they achieve the same level of success in managing people and targeting markets.

For my first visit to Japan in 1990, I had to prepare a presentation of the market that I was representing. At that time, I was representing only Ireland. I had read that in Japan the map of the world is laid out differently from what we are used to in Europe. In Europe, the United Kingdom is in the centre of the world map because the 0° longitude runs through Greenwich in London. This places Japan on the far right of the map. The Japanese map of the world places Japan in the centre, so that Europe in general and the British Isles in particular, are on the far left of the map. When I looked more closely at the Japanese map, I realised that from their point of view, Ireland was a small island nestled insignificantly in the top left corner of the world, not very far from another insignificant island called Iceland. I had read that many Japanese confuse the two islands because - for them - the only difference is one little letter. Knowing that I was going to speak before a multinational audience that included many Asians, I prepared a number of slides to show that Ireland was actually very close to Europe and that, in terms of size, it was actually bigger than some European countries better known in Japan, such as Holland. The explanation was appreciated by the audience, most of whom were reluctant to admit that they actually knew very little about Ireland. As for the Japanese who were confident that they knew Europe very well, they rarely acknowledged that their knowledge was confined to the five major markets, that is, Germany, UK, France, Italy and Spain which represent 75% of European demand. They believed that their presence in those five major markets automatically guaranteed a presence in the smaller European markets. For them, this was the Europe that counted: if they could gain a position in these markets, then they would have covered the continent. My opinion, based on fifteen years' experience, is that that this is the wrong approach. For most products, the competition and the costs of entry into the market are higher in the five major markets, and local brands of most products are preferred to imported goods. To set up a pilot or test market in one or more of the smaller European markets is comparatively easy, just as it is far easier to establish a brand that does not compete with national icons. For example, in Ireland, Toyota became the top selling car brand for many years. The company sponsored local sports' teams and advertised using local Irish settings. Although Ireland was a small market in overall European terms, it was where Toyota held its biggest European market share. In fact, during my time with Bridgestone in Ireland, our brand became the overall market leader in the tyre business and Ireland represented Bridgestone's highest market share among European countries. In the case of both Toyota and Bridgestone there was no competition from a national iconic brand, hence the success that can be achieved in a small market.

Well-managed Japanese or other Asian brands can reach a market share three times higher in the smaller markets than they can in the larger ones and at a fraction of the cost. In my early years in the European headquarters, my expertise in this area was used. However, as the European business grew and as top management regularly changed, understanding of how to tailor the business to fit the market was lost, and the old habit of treating Europe as one market took over again.

One of the greatest examples of this at Bridgestone was the Benelux market. In particular, the Belgian market is one of the most complex in Europe because it is fragmented by language and culture. The Flemish-speaking population in the north of the country, the German speakers to the east, and the French speakers in the south are culturally different even if they live in an area of only 11,787 square miles. In the early 90s, Bridgestone decided to merge the Belgian and Luxembourg sales operations with those in The Netherlands to create one company that would manage the three countries. The headquarters were located in Holland where the staff spoke Dutch but not French.

After several years, it became apparent that Bridgestone's market position in Belgium, particularly in the French-speaking south of the country, had dwindled and had become insignificant. The company revoked the decision to centralize management in one place, and divided the Belgian and Dutch companies again. With a newly-appointed Belgian to run the revived Belgian company, the business thrived and the Bridgestone brand gained a position equal to its European average.

However, once again, after yet another change of top management, the markets were merged again. This time, the Dutch and Belgian markets came under the management of the French company. The European CEO in charge at the time failed to understand, like many of those at his level of management, that the European reality was multifarious and demanded innovative responses. He believed, like others before him, that all Bridgestone's advertising in Europe should be in English. It seemed that all important decisions in Europe were constantly being made without sufficient understanding of the real market characteristics and that these inevitably lead to mistakes. The end result was low morale among local employees.

Ideas of Ethical Behaviour

In his management policy, Shinagawa as global CEO once talked about "doing the right thing in the right way". This reflection on values resonated with me. I believe that as human beings we know the difference between right and wrong, and that we live by codes of ethical behaviour. In business, we know that taking the easy route is not always what is best for the company. When faced with difficult business choices, "what would you do if you owned the company?" is often a good starting point for action. Framing the question in these terms usually helps to steer thinking towards "doing the right thing in the right way". In my experience, this has resulted in most people choosing to do that which would give the best result for the company instead of that would be the easiest to manage.

This philosophy was tested when an email arrived on my desk from someone using a false name. He presented himself as an ex-employee of one of our major competitors and said that he had worked in their research and development department for six years. He wrote that before leaving the company, he had copied his hard disk and had information about the company's new product strategy, including technologies, for the coming years. He added that he was willing to sell this information, and asked that his message be transferred to the relevant department.

The company he had worked for was Bridgestone's main competitor, a true global leader. It was clear that the information would give us a competitive advantage and help us overtake the competitor in the global race to be number one. I thought about our research and development teams, how they were investing huge time and resources examining the performance of the competitor's tyres. Surely I should leave it to the head of research and development to decide how to handle the offer. As I tried to work out what I should do, I thought about my training; I considered my ethical beliefs and Shinagawa's policy to, "Do the right thing in the right way". Finally, I chose three courses of action:

1. to not share this information with anyone else in the company
2. to not respond to the sender of the email
3. to inform the competitor that I had received the email.

My decision set in motion a chain of events whose effects were still being felt years later. The competitor company worked with their national police to set a trap for the "spy" who was unmasked and convicted of attempting to sell state secrets. The case was reported in the media and Bridgestone was widely praised for its ethical behaviour. As a result of the media coverage, customers contacted our offices to say how impressed they were and how the company would now be considered a preferred supplier. The impact on the brand value was immense. Subsequently, several leading companies came together to lobby for legislation that would protect trade secrets and establish a code of ethics that would regulate practice.

Meanwhile within Bridgestone, opinions differed about my handling of the situation. Many European employees were truly proud of my response and were happy to be a part of a company that would behave in this way. Others, including my CEO at the time, suggested that I had gone too far and that I should have ignored the email and not acted at all. Then there were those, some Japanese and some European, who believed that we had lost a great opportunity to outdo a competitor. They were the sort of people who believe that all is fair in war and competition, and that if we could have taken advantage of a competitor's security leak then we should have done so. I am convinced that the longer term benefits of ethical behaviour always outweigh the short term advantages that may be gained from situations like the one I have described.

Today, I have a conscience that is completely clear in relation to the incident. Some months later, members of highest management in Tokyo, whatever they may have thought at the start of the affair, sent me a message commending my response. They nevertheless did not use the incident as an example of best practice in their management training programmes. Consequently, I have concluded that diverging or even conflicting understandings of right and wrong within the company continue to confront each other.

The integrity with which I handled the spy case testified my goodwill and support of the founding principles of the Bridgestone company. It's unlikely that my behaviour would have been matched by a Japanese member of staff who found themselves in the same situation. I am sure that if a Japanese colleague had been faced with the same choice, he would not have acted before talking to his boss but he probably would not have wanted to create a problem for his boss, so the Japanese colleague probably would have ignored the original email. Handling the issue in that way would have created the least disturbance internally. However, it would have meant that the company failed to take a rare opportunity to testify to its high ethical standards. As a PR professional, I understood how seldom such opportunities arise, and how they can pay great dividends if handled correctly.

Austerity Need Not Apply to Everyone: Some are More Equal than Others

My time at the European headquarters straddled periods of economic growth and decline in Europe. The financial performance of the company fluctuated in time with the overall business environment. When there was a decrease in the company result, all departments and subsidiaries were directed to reduce their expenses by a given percentage for the remainder of the financial period. At some stage, this became so predictable that managers would plan to make their most important expenses early in the financial period so that they would avoid cuts in the later months. European managers would cancel discretionary expenses, meetings and business trips in an effort to curtail spending while Japanese managers behaved as if they were above such cutbacks.

One European CEO, who as usual was Japanese, always travelled in the highest flight class available. He would always use business class, or first class if it was available no matter what the financial situation. I recall that on two occasions I was travelling on the same flight as the CEO of Continental, a competitor of Bridgestone. He made a point of travelling economy class which impressed me because I admired his attitude and because it set the example of responsible behaviour that would have a knock-on effect for other members of his company. At Continental, no one below the CEO would even consider travelling in a class higher than economy. Meanwhile, at Bridgestone, middle and senior managers would try to find ways to travel business class or higher. They would delay booking their flight until the only seats available were in business class. On one occasion, I proposed that we should have a policy to travel on low fares airlines like Easy Jet and Ryanair. I even led by example by booking Ryanair flights for myself and two members of my team for a return trip to Rome. The cost at just over 300 Euros for the three of us represented a saving of 1200 Euros on the Brussels Airlines cost. However, my proposal to introduce a policy was dismissed with feeble excuses that flight times were not convenient or that the additional thirty minute travelling time to a different airport was not manageable.

The reality was that the top managers who were Japanese did not see cost saving as something in which they were implicated. In their view, and from their hierarchical standpoint, such measures applied only to the "staff". In the days when senior Japanese attended the Formula 1 rounds in Europe, they invariably stayed in five-star hotels in luxury suites with chauffeur-driven cars for the weekend. Privately, I questioned their purpose of attending the events at all, as the Formula 1 operation was handled by a separate subsidiary division called Bridgestone Motorsport. But, again from the point of view of executives who were on overseas assignments usually without their wives, attending events like Formula 1 was their way of asserting their intention of making the most of their European posting.

Feed that Ego

The belief in their self-importance amongst high-level managers at Bridgestone was best exemplified by Shimbashi when he arrived in Europe. He was a passionate follower of Formula 1, and insisted that he must attend all the European races that season. He justified this by arguing that it gave him an opportunity to meet customers who were at the races as corporate hospitality guests. The fact that most of those customers could not speak English was conveniently ignored.

Shimbashi arrived in Barcelona for the Spanish Grand Prix weekend and headed to the circuit to meet with Kawasaki, the head of Bridgestone Motorsport. Kawasaki had a problem and he knew he could get help from Shimbashi. A year before, at the end of the previous Formula 1 season, Bridgestone had given notice of its withdrawal as the tyre supplier to Formula 1. Kawasaki was therefore nearing the end of his association with Formula 1 racing and was not happy about it. He felt that he had nothing to lose in trying to change the decision that had been taken at the board level in Japan and, recognising an ally in Shimbashi, he decided to use him.

Kawasaki knew that Shimbashi's ego was easily stroked and so he spent the weekend taking Shimbashi from one Formula 1 team to another. Shimbashi sipped champagne with the team principals and met with famous drivers. He was entertained in the private offices of Bernie Ecclestone who insisted that Bridgestone was a much-needed partner, and was made to feel like a demi-god. Here he was, the CEO of Bridgestone Europe, mixing with the rich and famous from the Formula 1 world which he adulated. He posed for the media, and wallowed in the attention he received. Kawasaki, in the meantime, was telling journalists that Shimbashi had the power to change Bridgestone's decision to withdraw from Formula 1.

The following day, several leading newspapers announced that, "Shimbashi says Bridgestone should stay in Formula 1." At the time, I was head of Public Relations. I was soon receiving phone calls from the Tokyo office asking me to explain the news reports. How could I allow these reports when the final decision had already been made? Shimbashi tried to pass the reports off as bad reporting. My colleagues who had been in Barcelona recounted that he had simply fallen into Kawasaki's trap and allowed himself to be manipulated.

As the season progressed, Shimbashi continued to attend the Formula 1 race weekends and to enjoy the champagne lifestyle. At the Belgian Grand Prix, he hosted a party for all the members of the tyre supply team, even though they were not from his area of responsibility. He organised a barbecue for them, and gave a speech praising them for their outstanding work. He also repeated that the decision to leave Formula 1 was a bad one, and that if he had anything to do with it, the company would re-enter the sport at the earliest opportunity. Shimbashi had already stated very clearly to me that withdrawing from Formula 1 was the biggest mistake the company could have made. When I dared to disagree with him, arguing that leaving would save the corporation millions of Euros as part of the global cost-saving effort, he decided that henceforth my opinion on any matter was valueless. This was the beginning of a process that would lead inexorably to my departure from the company a year later.

Meanwhile, the champagne lifestyle of top executives like Shimbashi continued. The "do as I say and not as I do" style continued much to the dismay of the non-Japanese who were genuinely putting the company first.

Different Cultural Attitudes As Seen From The Top

When Mizutani took up his position of CEO in Europe, he knew it would be his last posting before retirement. He was old-fashioned in many ways, but was open-minded and a good listener if one could get time with him. After little more than a year in Europe, at a dinner of senior executives, Mizutani shared what he believed he had learned from his overseas postings, including this one, his first in Europe.

He said that he was fascinated by the difference in motivation that he had noticed in various offices around the globe. According to him, in Japan, if a manager wanted one of his team to do something, he just told them to do it; in the United States, the team members would do what was asked of them if the manager gave a financial incentive; in Europe, to his surprise, he found that when he asked his direct reports to do something, they first asked "why". He had learned that for Europeans it was essential to understand the reason for a course of action before they supported it. His insights remain valuable for any non-European company hoping to do business in Europe. Most Japanese managers with whom I worked never came to the same conclusion that Mizutani did. Even if they understood his theory, they remained unable to accommodate the needs of the European staff. They continued to issue instructions which they expected to be followed without question.

Chapter 5

Socialising

The Japanese with whom I interacted on many levels displayed a capability to behave very differently depending upon the event or the perceived status of the people with whom they are interacting. They could be extremely polite or unabashedly rude.

On the Golf Course

Because I am an avid golfer, I have often been invited to join Japanese golf competitions on weekends. I have to admit that it is not my favourite way to play golf. I prefer to start my game early in the morning and to finish by lunchtime. The Japanese make it a full-day event starting mid-morning and finishing mid-afternoon. A late lunch and drinks follow. As well, Japanese players enjoy betting on several competitions at the same time. They bet on everything from putting statistics to determining the nearest the pin or the longest drives. As a result, people like me, who may have finished a round of golf with the best score, found that they owed a lot of money for losing the sub competitions. Similarly, junior Japanese employees often affirm that they can play golf when, in fact, they only have a rudimentary knowledge of the game. They do this because golf is a game played predominantly by senior executives and the juniors aspire to be a part of this inner circle. A really able golfer can find themselves paired with a real beginner in a competition. The beginner will be tenacious which in most cases, is a quality; except when it slows the game down –as it always does. And when it slows the game down, it creates a backlog and queue throughout the whole golf course. I have had many experiences where paired with aspiring junior Japanese beginners I have had to assist them searching for lost balls, and taking ten or more shots on every hole but being oblivious to the angry stares from the following group. For the European participating in such a group, it is inevitably an embarrassing and frustrating experience and is best avoided.

A Private Dinner Party

After two European colleagues and I were appointed as vice presidents, the CEO, Mizutani invited us to dinner in his home together with our wives. We were aware that this was a very great honour. We knew that the Japanese invited each other to their homes, but this was the first time we had ever heard of a non-Japanese colleague being respected in this way.

Because we expected it to be a formal evening, we all dressed up: collars and ties and long dresses. When we arrived at Mizutani's beautiful house, we were greeted at the front door by both Mizutani and his wife. A series of very formal introductions followed and, with them, an exchange of bows. Mizutani's wife, in particular, was bending over more deeply than any of her guests. We were asked to remove our shoes and to select a pair of slippers from the row which was neatly lined up along the wall in the hall. None of us had anticipated this, and the women ended up abandoning their elegant high heels and having their long dresses sweep along the floor.

We spent some time together in the living room where Mizutani toasted our success with champagne. His wife disappeared into the kitchen. I was surprised that they had not engaged a caterer for the evening but, in fact, this helped us to relax and to feel that we were being welcomed as genuine guests in an unpretentious and informal setting.

We were soon invited to the dining table, which was set up in classic European fashion which meant that we did not have to sit on the floor. Mizutani's wife brought out the small bowls of Japanese food while Mizutani remained seated at the table all the while barking orders in Japanese. We could not see what she was doing wrong, but he was clearly dissatisfied. We all felt uncomfortable and yet when one of our wives offered to help, he quickly but politely refused.

The dinner began with two courses of typical Japanese pickles, raw squid and other exotic delicacies. Unlike my fellow guests, I had gained useful experience with Japanese food and table manners over my time working with the Japanese, but even I was surprised when the main course of noodles was served. Mizutani's wife was in the corner of the dining room, kneeling by a cooking apparatus on the floor, stirring various ingredients into a bowl. One at a time she filled bowls with noodles and brought them to the table. Each time, Mizutani greeted her with bristling criticism. Finally, without saying a word, she filled her own bowl and joined us. When the evening was formally over, we removed our slippers, put on our shoes, thanked our hosts, and bowed our goodbyes. Mizutani and his wife remained at the front door waving to us until we were out of sight.

At the end of the dinner and just as we were preparing to leave, we had posed together for a formal photograph in front of the family fireplace. A few days later, we each received a print of the picture with a note of thanks for coming to their home.

As we thought about the evening, we were most struck by the difference in culture that we had experienced. I had been prepared for much of what had greeted us: the formality, the photograph, the food itself. What surprised me was Mizutani's wife but particularly, his treatment of her. The way he spoke to her would not have been accepted by a servant in Europe, yet it seemed to be the norm in their home. To be served bowls of noodles from a woman crouched below us on the floor was unusual but, it was clear to us that, for her, it was not.

I have recounted the dinner to many people over the years, and I am always fascinated by their various reactions. Some people are astounded and quickly conclude that Mizutani and his wife simply did not know how to host a party. Others respond by saying that codes of hospitality are not universal and suggest that the opportunity to enjoy a privileged glimpse into the workings of a Japanese household should be experienced and enjoyed on its own merits.

Similar responses are expressed when considering the differences in the codes of doing business with the Japanese. Some people engage with the difference as if it were a confrontation. In this case, they judge the experience according to their own points of reference and often conclude that the Japanese way of doing business is problematic for them. Others are willing to engage with the codes without judgment and allow the experience to open them up to something new.

What is clear is that both the Japanese and the non-Japanese must allow for the fact that their codes are not the same. Both will encounter habits and customs that may be unsettling for them but if they want to work together successfully and develop a business culture that is respectful, these differences must be accepted or overcome.

Letting Their Hair Down

In spite of the formality that reigns during most Japanese events, it is quite astounding to observe what can happen when the Japanese lower their guard: Japanese parties can be very entertaining, at times they can be quite outrageous.

During my first year in Brussels, I attended a company party celebrating the New Year. A wide and diverse mix of Japanese and Europeans colleagues came together in a spacious room. There was a great deal of music and singing. Many of the party-goers were drinking heavily and getting progressively drunk. One young Japanese, by the name of Nishimoto, who was famous for his party routines, stood on a chair and launched into a Japanese song. As the song progressed, he began to remove his clothes. The crowd gathered and cheered him as he stripped down to his underpants. To my amazement, he whipped off his underpants as well, put them on his head like a hat and continued singing. The crowd roared. In the process, I got my first insight into the ease with which the Japanese shuffle their standards depending on the context they are in.

Even senior members of Japanese management in the room did not sanction his behaviour. It seemed to be an accepted fact that such excesses were inevitably part of a drunken party. I wondered what the reactions would be the next day when we were all back in our offices. The Europeans were amused and gleefully shared their stories about it; the Japanese behaved as if the incident had never occurred. Nishimoto later returned to Japan and continued to progress in his career.

On another occasion I visited a company-owned rubber plantation in Indonesia. There was a company guest house with private rooms and common eating and relaxing areas on the plantation. When we arrived, my colleagues, who were mostly American, and I were given a tour of the plantation and its state of the art facilities. Later, once we had checked into the guest house, we were informed that we were expected to have dinner with both the plantation manager and the finance director both of whom were Japanese. We gathered at the appointed time, moved quickly through the formal introductions and greetings, and took our places at our table where three bottles of hard liquor and several bottles of beer were served. We were tired and not in a mood for heavy drinking, but it was very clear that our Japanese hosts had been looking forward to our arrival as an opportunity to have a party. I have never seen a bottle of whisky disappear as quickly as I did that night. After enjoying a delicious meal, we were ushered into an entertainment room with its inevitable karaoke machine. More drinks were brought and our two jovial hosts continued to drink. The atmosphere quickened when we were asked to perform several solos or duets on the karaoke. It grew even merrier when the finance director began doing push-ups in the middle of the room in time to the music, first using two sturdy arms and then only one. His physical strength was impressive, but we were even more impressed by the fact that such a display could take place in the middle of a drinking party. The party continued until very suddenly, at exactly nine o'clock in the evening, the music stopped. Ishikawa, the Finance Manager, repeated, "Party over, party over". No time to finish our drinks: he was pointing at the door and it was clear that it was time to leave. The party was over. I soon realised that social activities, without exception, ended at 9 o'clock in the evening. I also understood why our hosts, unvaryingly, drank a great deal very quickly.

The following day, when we arrived at the plantation offices, we were met by Ishikawa. I smiled and asked him about his arms. His demeanour changed immediately and he shook his head disapprovingly. I was making a very serious mistake: I was bringing talk about a social occasion into the workplace. Again, I was being shown that context is everything for the Japanese. Drunken one-handed push-ups are perfectly acceptable in the party context but should never, can never, be mentioned anywhere else.

On yet another occasion, I was attending a global meeting in Tokyo. The meeting was scheduled to end on a Friday. Common practice is that visitors are hosted to a party that includes dinner, drinking and karaoke. This time the party was hosted in a private room in a restaurant. The group included about ten visitors from around the world and about ten local Japanese. Our host, Namiki-san, soon started the drinking games. Having grown up in Ireland, and been a rugby player for a few years, I had seen a fair share of drinking games but the speed at which people were expected to drink at this party shocked me. I had to be very creative about missing a round of shots and staying somewhat sober.

While our party moved into full swing, another party, hosted by the Human Resources department, was well under way in an adjoining room. From what we could hear through the paper screens, it was apparent that the participants were getting drunk, and just as I thought our party was ending and that I could look forward to escaping, the global head of Human Resources entered. He was delighted to find that our group was still there and insisted on meeting everyone in the room. At the same time, he ordered more drinks even though some of the younger Japanese were already having difficulty speaking coherently. No-one dared to leave the party for fear of offending the senior member of management who continued to order drinks until he was so drunk, he fell off his chair. I simply could not have imagined a European manager of his level in the same condition.

When the party finally ended, we spilled out onto the street. I watched as one of the young Japanese stumbled and sat down against a wall. He waved his hand in a gesture that told us very clearly that we should "please just leave". His colleagues were happy to oblige him. As they ushered us towards the waiting taxis, they laughed and moved on.

These and other experiences confirmed an unbridgeable difference between the Japanese and the Europeans. The ability of the Japanese to contextualize behaviour is impossible for Europeans. Many people have damaged their reputation and their careers by drinking too much, making rude comments or becoming too familiar with senior colleagues during a social event. In Japan, what happens outside the business environment stays outside the business environment. There seems to be no judgment connected to the drinking culture that is an integral part of the Japanese business environment.

Chapter 6

Planning and Budgeting

Mid Term and Long Term Planning

Almost all case studies of big corporations refer somewhere to long-term planning. If we look more closely, it's not always clear what this actually means. In some cases, it may be referring to a period as long as ten to fifteen years just as it could be considering a five-year horizon. Sometimes the five-year benchmark becomes a mid-term plan. In all cases, these plans become the base or reference point from which annual budgets are set. However, companies can be so focused on their long-term plans that they are unable to react quickly enough to the realities of the changing business climate. Long-term planning can become a trap.

The Japanese have a reputation for long-term planning. At Bridgestone, the idea that there should be a mid-term planning process was championed by Shinagawa both when he was the European CEO, and later, when he returned to Japan. The concept which he designed and that would be used to plan the company development for the following five years made perfect sense: to be effective the mid-term planning process requires a truly impressive depth of study and preparation. At Bridgestone, although the amount of time and resources devoted to the process represented a huge cost, the outcome was always a clear plan for the company's five year direction.

If there was a weakness in the system, it was that it required clear and effective communication and collaboration amongst complex webs of different divisions. This challenge was further complicated by the fact that the company was a global one and so geography also became a factor. Within each strategic business unit, the process required regular communication between the different departments. Manufacturing plans needed to support sales plans, and profitability depended on balanced selling prices and manufacturing costs. Assumptions had to be made and issued to all departments to cover projected costs, interest rates, staff numbers and labour costs. Therefore, the plan could not be adjusted easily when new circumstances arose, and changes from one year to the next were almost impossible to introduce.

Annual Budgets

A budget process was performed at Bridgestone twice every year. The budget for the following year was prepared between September and December. It encompassed all aspects of the business: from development to manufacturing and sales; from operating expenses to all supporting activities. A revised budget process was carried out between April and June and was supposed to take into account the reality of the first quarter which should have been reflected in the forecast for the second half.

The initial budget for each year derived from the mid-term plan and was set in stone. All divisions were instructed to set their budget at, or above, the level of the mid-term plan. In other words, proposing a reduced sales budget, if it was not included in the mid-term plan, would never be accepted even if the economic situation had changed dramatically.

Mid-term plans were very often set by a management team or CEO who was scheduled to leave his position and who, therefore would have no real responsibility for their achievement. If the sales and profit levels were unachievable, it was no matter to them because they would be far away when the results came in and could not be blamed for any failure to meet the targets. The European divisional managers who were not relocating had no choice but to accept unrealistic targets set by soon to be disengaged management.

I lived through various boom and bust cycles in the budgeting process. Bridgestone was a relative newcomer to Europe, but following its takeover of Firestone in 1988, the company gained a foothold in Europe as well as a network of local factories with research and development facilities. Moreover, it acquired a healthy market share (with the Firestone brand) in some of the European countries. This status raised confidence levels and led to aggressively optimistic growth plans for Europe. These, in turn, led to growth targets for market share which many experienced European managers, of which I was one, considered to be completely unrealistic. But we learned quickly that the targets could not be questioned: any suggestion that they were unachievable was met with dismissive indictments of complacency. If we were not willing to meet the challenge, then we should not be with the company.

By the end of my fifteen years in the European headquarters, the company's market share in the most important product category had hardly changed at all. There were many reasons for this but in spite of the "flat line" experience, the mid-term plan continued to indicate aggressive future growth expectations. Each year, the mid-term plan was revised, and the current year's achievement added, as well as one more year, the fifth year forward. Repeatedly, the only important change in the plan was the date. Another year of not meeting the target was recorded and a new one added, yet the unrealistic growth objectives remained. Each year, a new mid-term plan was written. The preceding year's flat line performance was acknowledged, and the growth line for the following years became more ambitious in an effort to catch up growth that had been planned but not achieved.

Every new CEO who joined headquarters in Europe was shocked to inherit a mid-term plan that was unachievable and to discover that he was powerless to change it. And yet, these very CEOs had to set up their next budget based on the unrealistic mid-term plan they had inherited. When the accumulated failures reached a point of total disconnect between the mid-term plan and the budget, top management in Japan allowed an extraordinary revision. This breathing space was a lifeline for the presiding European CEO, and provided an opportunity to come close to achieving the next budget. However, even after the revision of the first year of the five-year plan, the targeted growth remained elusive. In fact, the projected targets were never achieved.

Personally, I was always in favour of setting optimistic and challenging targets provided the necessary resources were in place. But there is a difference between optimism and dreaming. I often discussed my thoughts about these budgets with my European colleagues, and the sufficiently experienced among them also agreed on how unrealistic they were; and because they also knew that their potential bonuses would only be awarded if the company reached and/or passed its targets, morale dropped each time the budgets were set at ridiculous levels.

Vision or Dreams?

When I arrived in Europe, management was deep into the implementation of an earlier plan to grow the market share to a specified target figure over a five-year period. The targeted growth was high by any standards, reflecting the ambition of the company. Several of the European managers, were concerned that the sales targets were unattainable because the production capacity to supply the tyres simply did not exist. We were assured that there was nothing to worry about. We were told that supplying the volumes required by the sales divisions was the responsibility of the global supply division, including manufacturing planning. This was a classic example of the silo mentality that continuously choked the company. The fact that the market share set in the five-year plan in 1997 had still not been reached fifteen years later was proof that the European managers had a more realistic view of what was attainable.

Key Performance Indicators in Silos

I cannot be sure if the silo mentality is as bad in non-Japanese companies, but I am sure that wherever it exists, difficulties in communication also exist and lead to situations where managers remain focused exclusively on their own targets and key performance indicators or KPIs, and not on a company-wide view. Under the Shinagawa management, the company benefitted from his synoptic vision and his attempts to progressively dismantle the silos, but after his departure from Europe the silos quickly re-appeared. His successor had neither the vision nor the judgment to manage the organisation, and turned to other managers to run the company.

Key performance indicators (KPIs) became one of the popular management consultant buzz words in the early part of the 21st century. Outside consultants advised companies on the setting and monitoring of KPIs, and divisional managers were forced to set KPIs for everything, even for projects that could not be objectively measured. I believe in the principle of KPIs and that they have an important part to play in focusing the minds of the staff on clear objectives, but they should not be confused with normal performance measurement.

KEY means that something is critical to the success or failure of the organisation. All too often divisional directors struggled to find performance measurements that they could classify as KPIs. *PERFORMANCE* must be measurable, and *INDICATORs* point to a development towards the future.

In practice, I found that KPIs were not understood in the same way by those that set them, those that measured them, and those that had to achieve them. The fact that there was neither training nor agreement about what was meant by or expected from the KPIs, automatically led to different interpretations of the concept. The goals and priorities of the business and its divisions were understood differently throughout the company. I have seen departments set their divisional KPIs without reference to other important divisions, yet if the KPIs across the company are not aligned to common goals then it is impossible to achieve the over-reaching goals. This is precisely what was happening repeatedly at Bridgestone Europe.

Sales divisions would typically set targets of market share growth or sales volumes for a given period. A sales target is probably one of the easiest performance goals to set and measure, but it is arguable whether it is a key to overall company performance or an indicator for a future trend. What I found was that short-term sales goals forced the operating teams to focus only on those short-term goals and to neglect the importance of long-term business development. The most effective tool to reach a short-term sales target is pricing. However, short-term achievement of a sales target achieved through price discounting can create long-term damage to an overall company result because it can set a new lowest price level, and /or parallel sales across borders. Sacrificing longer-term development plans through the achievement of short-term sales goals was the way of life at Bridgestone. Some of the sales company managing directors were experts at using certain sales channels to sell quotas outside their territories, and in so doing, ruining another market and the total company result. They did not care because they were focused on, and were measured against, their own KPIs.

In order to reach the sales target, the sales department considers promotions and deals to increase the volume. Individual salesmen will have bonus targets for increasing their sales volume, and blinded by the market share KPI, prices will drop and with them, the gross profit percentage. So if one division achieves it's KPI it will lead to another division missing its own. I do not suggest that this behaviour is a monopoly of Japanese companies. In fact, I have seen this short-term thinking in many western companies, but what is particularly ironic when it occurs in Japanese companies is that they pride themselves on having a long-term view.

Across a company, conflicting KPIs can be at the heart of bad performance. Even though it seems that it would be a simple process to resolve such conflicts through more open communication and management co-operation, the silo mentality blocks this. One might ask the question, "So why didn't you do something about it?" More than once, I pointed to the misaligned KPIs as a core reason for our difficulties. Many of my European colleagues recognised the problem as did some of my Japanese colleagues, but convincing Japanese managers that their current way of operating might be wrong was always considered presumptuous and dismissed as disloyal.

Typically, the manufacturing plants were measured against their production volume and production cost. However, in the tyre industry, producing certain tyres is easier than producing others, so the plant would try to maximise the output of the tyres which were easier to produce. The fact that the sales divisions wanted or needed other product types to meet the market demand was ignored by those chasing their own performance measurements.

Issues Beyond Control

The tyre market in Europe is split into two seasons. The northern European climate demands that motorists fit winter tyres to their vehicles from November through March. When tyre companies plan their sales they have no idea whether or not there will be severe winter conditions. The earlier the snow falls, the more people change to or buy new winter tyres.

There were years in which the sale of winter tyres was greater than budgeted forecasts because of severe winter weather. At the end of these periods, management-level executives earned valuable bonuses. While fortunate for those involved, earning money thanks to the weather and not because of effort and competence was one of those factors that meant that the cycle of good and bad bonuses continued. Conversely, in years when Europe experienced a "green winter" the market demand could fall dramatically, and despite committed and additional efforts by the sales forces, targets and bonuses could just not be met. Strange as it may appear, some Japanese managers were known to blame their employees for the weather conditions when this was the case.

The European company was always classified as an overseas business unit by the Japanese. As such, it took a backseat to the domestic home market when major decisions had to be made. Furthermore, when currency exchange rates moved unfavourably against the Japanese yen, the supply of exported tyres from Japan was allocated to more profitable markets. This made a mockery of the budgeting and planning process. The short-term decisions to reallocate supplies to more profitable markets was understandable if focusing only on short-term goals, but it was incompatible with and could even be disastrous for the longer term business development plans at the subsidiary.

Stop and Go

In the tyre business, especially when building a supply chain to a vehicle manufacturer, it takes a long time to build a relationship. The customer has to trust that the supplier will deliver the right goods on time to the correct technical specifications, and that the supply commitment will be met. As well, there is also the issue of price negotiations, but price alone will never secure the business. At times when manufacturing output exceeded sales demand, the sales forces were under pressure to sell more, and to do this they invariably used price cutting as the tool to obtain the business. The supply-demand pendulum would swing towards a shortage of supply to meet demand and the less important customers would be told that supplies were no longer available.

Many of these customers might have changed from a previous supplier to Bridgestone and would have been lured into believing that their demand would continue to be supplied. They then found themselves without a supplier and unable to complete their production of trailers or vehicles until they could negotiate a new supply agreement with another manufacturer.

The European sales force went through many stop and go cycles of this type of business behaviour. Many of them left the company rather than confront customers with inevitable broken promises. One colleague recounted the story of visiting a trailer manufacturer to rebuild a business relationship. The managing director of the customer company insisted that no matter the offer, he would not re-enter a stop and go supply situation which had already created too much risk for his business and which only promised more of the same.

Analysis Versus Pragmatism

On another occasion, following an increase in the cost of raw materials Bridgestone was under pressure to increase selling prices. The Japanese directors reporting to me suggested that we compare our price position in each European market against our competitors, and from that analysis calculate a reasonable price increase. After having tried this approach several times before, I encouraged them to understand that the need to increase prices was immediate, that the analysis they were proposing would take too long and, that in any case, would be unreliable because we did not have the resources necessary to ensure a thorough study.

Beyond this, although I agreed that our current price structure was not ideal, I argued that we were at least established in the market and were actually selling. Therefore, any price increase would be starting from a position that was already accepted by the market. I also believed that the pressure to increase prices was probably also affecting our competitors and that they, too, would need to increase prices. Any analysis prepared at a time when all competitors were moving or changing their prices would be inconsistent. I pushed for an immediate price increase.

In one country in Europe where we were represented by a sole distributor, I saw an immediate opportunity. The price level at which we were selling into that market was low compared to other European markets, but Kobayashi, one of my sales directors insisted that we needed to examine the prices in that market even more than the others. After much discussion, I agreed that he should study the market prices there as soon as possible, and looked forward to seeing the result. In the meantime, I called the distributor to whom I explained the situation we were in and informed him that prices on all tyres would be increased by 3% effective the following month. The distributor responded that he preferred not to be confronted with the situation but that he understood and accepted. We implemented the price increase without any negative effect on our business. To this day, the thorough analysis of price levels against competitors in that market has not been carried out because of insufficient time and resources.

Pragmatism is not a word that I readily associate with the Japanese members of my team. Too many times, they hid behind a need to study or investigate data before making decisions. Often it disguised an inherent fear of taking risk and avoiding making any decision that could implicate them if anything should go wrong.

The Preparation Process

At headquarters, the team preparing the figures for the next budget period would start their work four months before each implementation date. The finance and administration departments were consumed with this work. Models were used to measure the impact of price and volume movements, but the studies were done separately for the manufacturing and sales departments with very little reference to each other. Looked at in isolation, the budget for the manufacturing division could look very impressive, but in reality it was often based on producing high volumes of simple products and lower volumes of the more complex products. Meanwhile, the sales divisions were instructed to prepare their budgets based on their demand analysis of the market place and based on unconstrained supply. This would have been a reasonable approach if the system allowed a later adjustment to match the production plans to the sales demand, but in practice this did not happen. To adjust production plans in a tyre plant takes many months, by which time the budget period would have passed.

Sales managers were able to calculate probable shortages in supply of certain product lines. Knowing that these products would be allocated to each country as a percentage of what had been requested, they increased their orders for those products, sometimes by as much as two-fold. This had the effect of making the market demand for those products appear even higher, and these figures would be fed into the longer term production planning. So in year N supply was 80% of the real demand and in year N+2 the supply could be 180% of the real demand for the same product item.

The unfortunate combination of departments that functioned in isolation and managers that were constantly changing clouded the real situation even further. Moreover, each manager was a prisoner of his budget. Whether realistic or not, his objective was to achieve his budget. This invariably led to a conflict between short-term and long-term goals. Achievement of long-term goals often called for investment in advance. Acquisition of businesses, expansion of premises, hiring of additional staff were all included in the budget as part of a long-term plan. However, achievement of short-term profits was easier if planned expenses were delayed until after the budget period. Managers, who knew they would only be in the position for a short time and who were determined to get their bonuses, would sacrifice long-term development plans for their short-term gain.

Fixed Commitment Regardless of Circumstances

When the global recession of 2008 hit Europe, a budget had already been signed off by the top management in Japan. At the same time, a new Japanese CEO and a senior vice president were both appointed to the European company where they opened the books and discovered the targets against which they were to be measured.

Every day, new lower forecasts were being submitted from car manufacturers, truck manufacturers, and tyre dealers. Demand was falling fast. The new executives were warned that their job was to manage the company and its targets regardless of changing circumstances. With sales falling fast, all the company's warehouses were soon full to capacity and additional warehouse space was needed. Meanwhile, the factories continued to pump out finished goods as the manufacturing division set about reaching their production targets as budgeted.

In due course, and far too late, the factories had to be shut down temporarily to try and regain a balance between supply and demand. The cost of the shut downs and the additional warehousing was enough to push the company into a loss-making situation. The new

CEO, Kikuchi, was blamed by the global chairman for the situation without taking into account the vastly changed circumstances that had precipitated the crisis. Kikuchi, fighting against the negative forces, and trying to rectify the situation, had implemented initiatives and processes that made the company leaner and better able to handle short-term changes. The results appeared in the bottom line the month he was repatriated to Japan with a record of failure. Meanwhile, his replacement arrived and took credit for the turnaround in the company performance.

Salary Cost Control

The Human Resources department was charged with the responsibility of keeping salary levels under control and it set the guidelines that were necessary to do so. However, in a company with a high staff turnover, new or recent recruits regularly arrived. It was also a habit in the company to recruit people at as low a salary as possible with the promise that once they had proven themselves, their salary could be increased to reflect the actual market level for the position. The problem was that even the Human Resources department had a high staff turnover and within a year or two, everyone except the recruit, had forgotten that his salary level had been set deliberately low, and that the guidelines for salary increases in the mid-term plan did not allow exceptional increases. This practice, which occurred regularly, was actually a contributing factor to high staff turnover.

I learned that the optimal time for an individual to negotiate salary levels was at the time of initial employment negotiations. Employees who joined the company at low salary levels got trapped at low levels. Even subsequent promotions, if they occurred, were calculated from the base level at which the individual was working. It was the mid-term plan guidelines that created the trap from which successive European managers were unable to escape.

Budget Presentations

The most dreaded period of the year, was the ten days during which each subsidiary presented its budget for the following year. The day started at 8 o'clock with a succession of subsidiary company managers presenting budget proposals in a room filled with representatives from each department who were responsible for evaluating how each was aligned with company policy in their area. The final presentation of the day would usually be made around 6 o'clock when senior management would begin another meeting to review all the presentations. Depending on the CEO, these meetings could often run late into the evenings. It was not uncommon for the day to end as late as 10 pm.

After a week of this, many of the head office managers were burned out and unable to muster the same attention as at the beginning of the week. At the same time, their email traffic mounted up and other routine jobs accumulated. Nevertheless, the succession of managers and their presentations continued relentlessly. The official language was English but many of the presenters had very strong accents which made it difficult for the audience, even for native English speakers like me, to follow everything. I often wondered how much was understood by the Japanese. They focused on the figures, but could not possibly have understood the explanations that were provided.

The budget process was a huge burden on everyone in the company but especially for the accounting and finance department. They had to consolidate all the budgets to produce a comprehensive company picture. Every day, top management would make changes and the accounting department would have to rework all the figures to reflect them. If the final result was not in line with expectations or targets, they had to rework the models until they provided figures that the senior managers wanted. This would lead to revised instructions to the subsidiaries and could include an expense cut, a headcount reduction, a change in sales volume or a price change. Often, the instructions were disconnected from the business reality and achievable outcomes; their only purpose was to build a budget on paper that was theoretically acceptable.

The staff turnover in the accounting and finance department was higher than the company average. Several of the accountants after experiencing the work overload of the budget process, moved on to other companies.

Political Opportunities

The ten days of presentations were also an opportunity for ambitious individuals to make an impression. It was the only period in the year when middle managers could be in the same room as the CEO and other board members for long periods. The politically savvy among them, having examined the presentations in advance, would prepare questions for the presenters. Their objective was to impress the top management with their business understanding; those with the highest ambitions would comment and ask questions about topics outside their field of responsibility in order to demonstrate their wide business acumen. When these political manoeuvrings began, they were often followed by comebacks from other ambitious department heads who wanted to prove that they were equally astute. Unless the CEO took control, meetings easily degenerated into nothing more than sessions of political posturing.

For the subsidiary company managers, the process was about getting a conservative budget passed. They manipulated price assumptions; they maximised operating costs and headcounts because if a conservative budget could be passed, the team could earn generous bonuses. Some managers mastered this approach while others, especially the newer ones, were forced into accepting sales targets and price levels that would prove unattainable. For others, it was about buying time. If they could give the Japanese management the budget that they wanted, regardless of its feasibility, they had effectively bought six months during which the situation could change to make life easier for them. Frequently, it was a change of CEO or other top managers that would alter circumstances.

When the company budget was finally fixed, the process of presenting it to the global board in Japan began. The Japanese management in Europe would lock themselves in a room for a week to prepare their presentation in Japanese. Four or five of them, headed by the European CEO, would then head to Tokyo to present the European budget in two hours. Once accepted and approved by the global committee, all efforts were geared to its achievement.

My extensive years in a Japanese company have conditioned me to accept the importance of a meaningful budget. It is essential that the managers know their targets and limits, and that they have a benchmark against which to measure their performance. What I think presents the most difficult challenge to non-Japanese is the actual process of preparing budgets. In a company where the divisions operate in silos, and where cross-company communication is already a problem, preparing a budget can become an end in itself. Employees whose skills and talents are in other areas can find themselves locked into a budget preparation process while, in the meantime, the management of the day-to-day business imperatives is neglected. Similarly, when a long budget process results in targets in which the implementing teams have no confidence, then the process has failed, and the budget is no longer meaningful.

Closed for Business

The budget, once fixed, left no flexibility for unforeseen business opportunities. It gave the top Japanese management an easy answer when one of the Europeans proposed a business opportunity. Rather than considering the proposal, they could reply, "Sorry, it's not in the budget" This was the standard answer to any proposal that involved an investment or an expense. In fact, over the years, it became clear that any business ideas that required investments or major expenses were only ever generated from the Japanese network. These colleagues socialised together and explored ideas in a relaxed way. Non-Japanese had no access to this network and their ideas were automatically met with resistance from the outset.

Of course, there were exceptions. Occasionally, a European could convince the management to make an investment that was outside the budget plan, but it had to be a "no brainer" and even then had to be approved by a higher authority in Japan. This approval process explained the reluctance of Japanese management to listen to proposals from the non-Japanese. A business idea needed to be thoroughly researched and analysed before being proposed upwards. While this is understandable, the missing link for the non-Japanese was the exploratory stage. An idea is born out of a hypothesis or a concept. The Japanese could discuss scenarios and possibilities among themselves socially. The Europeans were locked out of this step; their ideas could only be introduced formally.

Chapter 7

Corporate Philosophies and Social Responsibilities

In the early part of the 21st century it became a trend among big corporations to issue a corporate philosophy, usually published on the company website, which was quickly becoming the reference point for anyone searching for information about the company. In the wake of the Enron scandal, corporations focused on communicating a positive image to investors and to society in general. I expect that consultancy firms specialising in helping corporations develop their corporate philosophies made vast sums of money at this time. However, many corporations ended up with statements about their corporate philosophies that differed only very slightly from each other.

From my experience of both presenting our company to groups of new European recruits and listening to their comments and questions, I learned that an employee's belief in the company and its philosophies is important to earn their engagement. They are not easily convinced by glossy brochures and lofty statements accredited to the President of the company. They expect to see and experience the company philosophy in their daily working lives. If the daily experience is different from the stated philosophy an educated and competent European will move on to another company. The Japanese managers never appreciated this. They were so conditioned by their own engagement that they neither questioned any apparently false assertions nor connected the departure of European employees to inconsistencies in the company philosophy.

Writer Josh Spiro (2010) defines company philosophy as *"a distillation of its culture or ambiance into a group of core values that inform all aspects of its business practices"*, [11]

Until recently, in Europe, it has been rare to encounter mission statements that include a "service" component whereas in Asia it has

---

[11] Spiro, J., 2010, 'How to Create a Company Philosophy', available at: http://www.inc.com/guides/create-a-company-philosophy.html, accessed on 6 May 2011

been very common. For example, Samsung's stated mission is, "To devote our talent and technology to creating superior products and services that contribute to a better global society."[12] Mission statements often capture a company's core values.

Bridgestone's current mission statement, "Serving Society with Superior Quality" derives from an earlier version which was, "Serving Society with Products of Superior Quality". The focal point of the revised mission statement shifted from the "product" to its "quality". The company commits to doing more than merely supplying a useful object; it pledges to be a force for the good. Bridgestone developed a whole program to expound this philosophy. They called it *The Bridgestone Way*, just as Fujitsu had created *The Fujitsu Way* and Toyota, *The Toyota Way*. All of them say essentially the same thing; all of them contain an impressive list of statements and guidelines meant to underline the core values of the corporate brand. But all of them are so alike in form and content that it is often difficult to tell one from the other: they sacrifice the specific and the extraordinary for the generic and the ordinary. If it is true that the nature, role, and function of core values are a central part of the value foundation of a corporate brand, then the particular should be made clear; that which distinguishes one brand from another should be made transparent and clear. Instead, deliberate "sameness" seems to be the operating principle amongst Japanese companies.[13]

Just as it is important for companies to differentiate their corporate brand image from each other, it is equally important to differentiate their products from those of their competitors. This is especially true for products which are borderline commodities. For consumers, except for specialists, tyres are black and round. My long years of experience at Bridgestone taught me the many ways that tyres can differ from each other; they also taught me that reaching consumers with this message is always an uphill struggle.

Japanese management repeatedly spoke about the importance of brand value and it was generally agreed that differentiating the brand

---

[12] The Philosophy of Samsung,
http://www.samsung.com/be/aboutsamsung/corporateprofile/valuesphilosophy.html
[13] Mats Urde, (2003) "Core value-based corporate brand building", European Journal of Marketing, Vol. 37 Iss: 7/8, pp.1017 - 1040

was an essential goal of advertising and communications campaigns. There was always consensus that increasing brand awareness, especially in undeveloped markets, was critical, just as it was always agreed that familiarity with the brand name alone was not enough. Finally, there was agreement that it was crucial for the brand to be perceived to have value. These principles closely matched my own: so far so good.

I learned, however, that Japanese understanding of brand development differed greatly from the European one and that brand promotion, and in particular advertising, is a vastly different experience in Europe and Japan. In spite of being aware of these differences, Bridgestone persisted in promoting its domestic values and approaches without considering the impact of the differences inherent in the European markets. As a consequence, millions of Euros were wasted on ineffective marketing.

Corporate Social Responsibility

In 2007, an official project to promote Bridgestone's concept of CSR was launched. A special office was set up in the Tokyo headquarters to lead a global effort to improve the company's performance in areas that included, care for the environment, responsibility to investors, to suppliers and customers, and to employees and their families.

When the project was rolled out to the European business unit, it was welcomed by the European employees who believed that the initiative would position Bridgestone as a leader in the relatively new field of corporate social responsibility, and that it would improve the profile of the company and the brand globally. It soon became clear however, that there are different interpretations of what CSR means and this resulted in some interesting outcomes.

The European Commission defines CSR as *"a concept whereby companies integrate social and environmental concerns in their business operations and in their interaction with their stakeholders on a voluntary basis"* [14]. But in the USA, CSR is associated with the idea of

---

[14] A renewed EU strategy 2011-14 for Corporate Social Responsibility, Brussels, 25.10.2011
COM(2011) 681 final

philanthropic practice by profit- making enterprises, while in Japan; it implies a concern for ethical behaviour by companies.

The findings of a university study in Japan prior to the launch of Bridgestone's concept stated that,

Corporate Social Responsibility, CSR is currently a fashion in Japanese business society. More Japanese companies have set up division of CSR and published CSR reports since 2003. However, it is not first time that corporate social responsibility, or social responsibility for corporate executives is noticed in Japanese business society. When the Japanese society began to industrialize, some Japanese companies, or business people recognized that they were a social institution. CSR, the relationship between business and society, is a subject of study of business administration from long ago. When the Japan Society of Business Administration was founded, Teijiro Ueda, who was a famous scholar of business administration in Japan, filled the post of the chief editor of "Business and Society". On other hand, companies do not recognize that they have sociality and most of them operating business in the domestic and oligopolistic market, operate as before and cause trouble in the society. [15]

I am reminded of the many social activities introduced by Bridgestone in Japan under the management of Shojiro Ishibashi, the founder of the company. His idea of "Serving Society with Superior Quality" was his legacy to the company. He provided housing for factory workers; organised and supported all kinds of sporting activities for the workers and their families; invested in the protection of natural areas, and invested in the arts including the building of a remarkable art gallery, now located next to the Bridgestone head office in Tokyo and open to the public.

It was a powerful foundation on which the company could build and the brand be developed. My engagement with Bridgestone and my long commitment to the company was inspired by the principles and values of Shojiro Ishibashi. I know many other Japanese and European colleagues who were equally motivated by this history and dedicated

---

[15] Nobuyuki DEMISE, Meiji University, Tokyo, Japan, CSR in Japan: A Historical Perspective

themselves to continuing the same values. However, over the years of rapid expansion and international growth of the company, these important values were lost. There were too many members of the company that did not get the chance to see, learn and understand the real Bridgestone culture.

Old Values in a New Package

In the year 2000, soon after the recall of Firestone Tyres (a brand of the Bridgestone group) in North America, a disaster that could have bankrupted the company, top management decided to try and reintroduce what they called the *essence of the company*. The thinking was that by going back to the roots of the company and linking back to its basic values, the global network of employees would reconnect with its culture and values. The idea was good but failed.

In each global business unit, ambassadors of *The Bridgestone Way* were appointed to lead training programs for employees throughout the organisation. As I was one of the employees who were perceived to have understood the core values of the company, I was used extensively in the European training programme. Although I wondered about the real purpose of the training after I learned that Toyota had introduced a similar program called *The Toyota Way*, I nevertheless felt that any training that could help to build employee engagement and a belief in the company would have my full support.

Several of my European colleagues joined me in rolling out the project, and it was soon clear and recognised globally that the European training team had committed fully to the project and that their implementation was the best in the world. I was proud of this. However, I realised how little the members of the line management above us had committed and, in fact, how little they understood the values they were being asked to communicate and advocate for. It was clear from the policy documents issued by the global CEO that top management was wholeheartedly behind the project, but the next level of management, including the level of European CEO, showed little evidence of sharing the enthusiasm. Several times, *The Bridgestone Way* ambassadors and I tried to convince the European CEOs that they should contribute to the project by speaking at some of the internal training sessions. None ever did. I thought that it would be more valuable for European employees to hear about the culture of the company from high-level Japanese colleagues than to hear it from another European. At the same time, their visible engagement in the program would demonstrate personal commitment. They never came forward. Over time, it became clear that the Japanese management below the C suite just did not buy into the project and, by inference, that they did not share my affinity with the principles of the founder.

The ambassadors continued their work but without the support and involvement of any of the Japanese management in Europe. I pointed out my concern to senior Japanese but there was no concrete or meaningful response. They would neither agree nor disagree. They would gently nod their head to confirm that they could hear what I was saying, but would not engage in any debate on the subject. It was a habit of the Japanese that I never got used to.

That *The Bridgestone Way* failed to inspire the global workforce was confirmed by a global employee survey which also revealed that the complexity of the supporting materials was a factor in the failure. Management's response to the survey results was to introduce *The Bridgestone Essence* which was a simplified version of the former program. The last paragraph of the introduction to the revised document announced that, "We can change the world through our products, services and corporate activities-if we all come together-if we all unite around The Bridgestone Essence" [16]Once again, the lack of support from the Japanese managers was enough to kill the initiative. Shimbashi, the European CEO at the time that it was introduced, approved the distribution of training materials among the employees but was not willing to invest in any other tools to promote *The Bridgestone Essence*. He dismissed the idea of online training which I had proposed. For him, as long as the materials were distributed, the box on the checklist of required actions could be ticked. No further management time would be allocated to it.

Linking Corporate Philosophy and CSR

Company philosophy was at the core of its approach to CSR. If the company really espoused the philosophy of *The Bridgestone Essence*, CSR practice and projects would derive naturally from it. The

---

[16] The Bridgestone Essence 2011

Bridgestone approach was to identify twenty-two issues to be addressed under the umbrella of CSR, and to set up a CSR committee to lead the projects in every subsidiary around the world.

The framework for the company's approach to CSR was in place and the European employees waited eagerly to see the results of their efforts. A year later, a document explaining the importance of CSR was circulated. Management policy, which was reviewed twice a year, included a section explaining that CSR was to be integrated into the business plans of each division. Nothing else happened.

A review of the original twenty-two topics included in the document shows that the company, like many other Japanese companies, identifies the following as the key CSR activities:

1. to secure stable profits
2. to comply with laws, regulations and company policies
3. to make ethical decisions that implement better business practices
4. to prevent risks and develop standards that help the business return to its normal operations as quickly as possible after an emergency occurs
5. to build effective communication structures that address the needs of both the local community and Bridgestone's business
6. to actively pursue effective communication with various stakeholders
7. to ensure continuous improvement of corporate governance.

Most western businessmen would consider these goals as basic "must dos" to survive in business and would not consider them to be specifically CSR topics. However, the Japanese view is different and these topics are considered as the fundamentals of CSR.

Diversity

Respect for diversity is also one of the twenty-two CSR topics. The European interpretation of this was that both Japanese and non-Japanese colleagues should be treated with respect and that they should enjoy equal opportunities; that women should be afforded the same career opportunities as men. In reality, the more senior positions in the European company were filled by Japanese, and in 2011, the highest-ranking woman in the organization was at the level of Senior

Manager, two steps below Director. Seth Friedman suggests a sociological reason for this:

With little to inhibit companies, they engage in blatant discrimination. One woman who worked in television wrote "It is still a grim reality in the office that men, while flattering women as "shokuba no hana" [office flower] hinder those who want to work for life and selfishly plan to use women as tea servers and sub-workers." Another woman, seeking to return to work after childbirth, was told, "Being a wife and mother is the best thing for a woman." Another woman commented "...it's the same in all professions. Japanese men really believe that women are inferior... [17]I have already discussed the mismatching of KPIs. It was also common that stated objectives, like these CSR issues, did not match other objectives in the company. For example, respect for age diversity meant that one should not discriminate against older employees or older applicants. Yet, at the same time that this principle was being heralded, a decision to lower the average age of employees was being made because younger employees cost less. A token representation of older employees was maintained as an illustration of the respect for the principle of age diversity but, at the same time, the end target remained unchanged: reduce the overall average age of the company.

Care for the Environment in CSR

In Japan, Bridgestone announced that it was supporting the World Wildife Fund's lake conservation project at Lake Biwa.

Lake Biwa - Sustainable Environment for Local Communities

This project aims to create a model for a sustainable community which will help people enjoy the natural benefits of Lake Biwa, a Global 2000 Ecoregion. To achieve this, the project aims, in partnership with local stakeholders, to renew local people's interests and understanding of the local lake-based culture and raise awareness of the problems caused by invasive species. [18]

It was a direction that everyone was expected to emulate. Although

---

[17] Women in Japanese Society: Their Changing Roles. Seth Friedman. December 1992
[18] http://wwf.panda.org/about_our_earth/ecoregions/lake_biwa.cfm

similar opportunities were sought in Europe, all were considered prohibitively expensive by European top management and dismissed. By the end of 2011, no project had been initiated by the Bridgestone Europe office and, in spite of the annual budget allocating a small amount to CSR activities, nothing was spent on them.

What emerged over a four-year period was that compliance with local laws and tax regimes was far more important to the Japanese than other components of CSR. The Japanese often referred proudly to the amount of taxes they paid, and Bridgestone's CSR projects focused more on regulatory compliance than on environmental compliance or social integration and community relations.

My training and business ethics prepared me to believe that such regulatory compliance would be taken for granted and that, in particular, a company founded on the philosophy of Shojiro Ishibashi would automatically comply with all regulations. This proved to be yet another naïve assumption.

Regulatory Compliance and CSR

The Enron scandal of 2001 and the resulting loss of trust in large corporations led to the Sarbanes Oxley Act (SOX) in America. The legislation, named after Senator Paul Sarbanes and Representative Michael Oxley, came into force in 2002 and introduced major changes in the regulation of financial practice and corporate governance, and set a number of deadlines for compliance.[19] The legislation was designed to ensure the regulatory compliance of corporations and introduced several new regulatory obligations.

In Japan, the Internal Control Committee of the Business Accounting Council of the Japanese Financial Services introduced the Japanese version of SOX, called J-SOX, which defined very strict rules for all listed companies in Japan in an attempt to ensure corporate compliance. The implementation of J-SOX required huge resources worldwide but a close look at the "measures" that were taken reveals that little was actually achieved. The exercise was reduced to a series of "ticking boxes" that led to management reports that suggested that the stated measures had been achieved.

---

[19] A Guide To The Sarbanes – Oxley Act http://www.soxlaw.com/

One such project was the implementation of a security policy. The level of information security in a company is important to protect the company from losing control of important information and safeguarding trade secrets. I was asked to ensure that all forty subsidiary companies in the European group accepted the written security policy. By signing an acceptance form, they were declaring that the rules in the security policy were being applied in their area of responsibility.

The security policy, comprising four separate policies, was eighty pages long and was written inEnglish. There were no translations into other European languages. Most of the local managers who received the policies struggled to read them but signed them nevertheless. A small number raised concerns that the policies did not reflect the security standards in their company. Finally, as a compromise, it was agreed that by signing the policies they accepted them as the target security level and nothing more.

This meant that at head office the J-SOX team had a file with forty documents confirming that the security policy was rolled out to all subsidiary companies. An audit ratified this. I became increasingly frustrated that in spite of collecting lots of documents and ticking boxes, the level of information security in the company was not changing. I managed to set up an e-learning program to train employees on good security practices and to implement a security badge system for employees and visitors to the European headquarters, but when I proposed encrypting laptop computers, the idea was rejected because of its high cost. However, even a low-cost procedure to classify documents by confidentiality ranking, which I also proposed, was blocked for unclear political reasons.

Realising that this was probably the reigning approach in Japanese companies, I was not surprised to read about the demise of Olympus which, as a Japanese listed company, had been obliged to comply with J-SOX rules as of 2008 but which had nevertheless been able to cover-up its fraudulent activities even from its own auditors.

Some may argue that the introduction of the Financial Instruments and Exchange Act in Japan –known by many as J-SOX thanks to its similarity to the US Sarbanes-Oxley Act – was intended to increase transparency, foster good corporate governance practices and stem the rate of high-profile corporate failures in Japan. Prior to the implementation of J-SOX in late 2007, fraudulent financial reporting by some Japanese companies appeared to be rife, while in 2005 around 14% of listed companies were forced to issue financial restatements. However, as the Olympus accounting scandal has shown, J-SOX seems to have failed in its goals - or rather government officials have failed to enforce it.

Shozaburo Jimi, Japan's minister of state for financial services expressed his concern that the incident had brought into question the fairness and transparency of the Japanese financial markets and has promised that, where there are doubts of violations of the Financial Instruments and Exchange Act (FIEA), the Securities and Exchanges Surveillance Commission (SESC) will undertake all necessary actions, including rigorous investigation and surveillance. Jimi also called on the Japanese Financial Services Authority to assess whether improvements need to be made to FIEA and their implementation. Key areas to be investigated include whether measures to achieve effective corporate governance for individual companies are sufficient and whether listing rules and disclosure regulations need to be reviewed to clarify the role and the degree of independence of independent directors currently required by exchanges. The FSA is also tasked with assessing why external auditors were unable to uncover the fraud, and whether any measures need to be taken by it and the Japanese Institute of Certified Public Accountants to improve auditing procedures to better deal with accounting fraud in the future. [20]

During my fifteen years at the European headquarters, I was privy to many highly confidential matters where the company had opportunities to act fraudulently; I never witnessed any such behaviour. I am confident that the company complied fully with all relevant laws and regulations. In fact, Bridgestone revised its corporate governance structure in order to strengthen its compliance. It was this conviction that the company was committed to good governance, especially at the highest levels in Japan, that kept me engaged with the company even when my faith was severely tested.

---

[20] Olympus scandal – a failure of J-Sox? subscriber.riskbusiness.com

And it was tested when I understood that management considered corporate governance and compliance the only important component of its CSR program. For me, caring for society and making efforts to improve the lives of real people is as important, if not more important.

Double Standards

Towards the end of my time at Bridgestone, mainland Europe endured the longest spell of severe winter weather in a generation. This led to an exceptionally high demand for winter tyres. The demand was so high that there was soon a shortage of them on the market. Companies made additional production runs and shipped out many more tyres than they had forecast. The result was that the tyre companies recorded unusually high sales and good financial results for the last quarter.

European motorists struggled with the conditions and there was an increase in traffic accidents on the dangerous roads. At the same time, the media was questioning why tyre manufacturers were not meeting the higher demand. As the person responsible for media relations, I replied that our company had manufactured additional tyres and shipped out more than our commitments to dealers everywhere. While I spoke in good faith, I subsequently discovered that Shimbashi, the CEO had suspended deliveries as soon as we surpassed the projected sales results for December. He had decided to keep back orders so that our office could get a good start in the following year's sales.

From a business point of view, I can understand the logic of his decision. I can even recall that during my period running a sales organisation we would review the order books at the end of every period to manage a smooth allocation of business and logistics. However, knowing that motorists were stranded or incurring accidents and injuries because winter tyres that we could have supplied easily were not available, went against everything I believed in. We could not have solved the shortage for everyone everywhere, but we kept thousands of winter tyres in our warehouses at a time when our customers needed us to prove our commitment to the idea of corporate social responsibility. The company's behaviour had put motorist's security at risk for the sole purpose of achieving timely financial results.

I later learned that Shimbashi had discussed the consequences of his decision to hold back inventory with other Japanese members of the management team but he had neglected to discuss it with Europeans. It was a safe option for him because none of the Japanese would challenge his ideas. The fact that the decision was contrary to one of the company's stated CSR objectives, that is, "to promote safe driving that is free of traffic accidents" was never an issue for him or for those who advised him. My conscience told me that Shojiro Ishibashi, the founder of the company, would have shared my indignation. He would have put his responsibility to society above his wish for a smooth business result. Shimbashi's decision underlined my belief that there was an enormous gap in understanding of the corporate philosophy among senior management in the company.

Even while the harsh winter conditions endured throughout Europe and as he continued to make his business decisions, Shimbashi issued his management policy for the New Year. He mentioned the importance of every divisional head taking CSR into consideration in their actions throughout the year, and he did as he was required to do: he re-iterated the importance of CSR. Once again, however, he had ignored the actual meaning of his own words.

Any person who is considering joining a big corporation should investigate the company's CSR policies and practices, to ensure that any suspicion of flagrant violations of social responsibility is unfounded. Assessing a company's ethical behaviour is as important as considering the benefits package when a decision to work for them is being made: it is impossible to sustain one's engagement and commitment to a company that does not reflect one's ethical standards.

Making a Real Difference

Fortunately for the company, elsewhere in the corporation there were divisions that worked specifically on projects that demonstrated true social responsibility. The Bridgestone Americas business unit sponsored several active programs promoting everything from "Keep America Clean" to safe driving for teenagers. One of their more important activities, which I had the good fortune to witness, involved the company's natural rubber plantation in Liberia in West Africa.

Liberia formed a relationship with the Firestone rubber company in 1926 when Harvey Firestone, the founder of the Firestone Rubber company, leased a large tract of land and planted thousands of rubber trees there. It became the biggest single plantation of rubber trees in the world. When Bridgestone bought over Firestone in 1988, the rubber producing facility in Liberia was a part of the package. Liberia had suffered from a military coup and subsequent economic collapse during the 1980s, and by the early '90s it had descended into a fierce civil war which lasted fourteen years. Firestone managed to maintain a skeleton operation throughout the war but most of the houses, hospitals, schools and facilities on the plantation were destroyed.

When relative peace returned at the end of 2004, Firestone's company in Liberia, under the management of Bridgestone Americas, began rebuilding the rubber producing facility. When the people of Liberia elected their new President, Ellen Johnson Sirleaf in 2006, the world's media once again turned its attention to this small West African republic. Several journalists who visited Liberia were shocked to find a capital city with no running water and no electricity, and a population with more than 80% unemployment. They also soon learned that the biggest employer in the country was Firestone's Natural Rubber Company with almost 6,000 employees. The media took a closer look at Firestone's facilities and reported appalling findings. They discovered local families living in mud huts; workers earning less than three dollars a day, and alleged cases of children being used to collect rubber. When these reports reached the magazines, radios and television screens of Europe, they created negative press and critical customer reaction towards Bridgestone.

At the time, I was in charge of public relations in Europe and this onslaught was becoming a bigger problem by the day. When I read the reports and watched the TV programs, I began to seriously question the corporate values of my employer. I was not willing to continue to work for a company that could act in such a manner. In 2006, I made my first of three visits to Liberia. I needed to see for myself what was really happening there and to ascertain if there was any truth in the reports. I quickly realised that context was important. In a country with so few resources, Firestone was providing jobs for 6,000 workers.

Fourteen years of civil war had prevented the housing program from building new homes, and when I arrived several home building projects were already underway to replace the worst of the old housing. New schools had been opened for workers' families whose children were entitled to free schooling. The teachers, paid by Firestone, were operating two shifts in each school to cater for the huge number of children taking lessons, and more schools were under construction. A hospital run by Firestone was being rebuilt and two other temporary hospitals had been commissioned. I also learned that the basic wage of around three dollars a day was a good salary in the Liberian context. One of the most alarming legacies of the civil war was the presence of groups of armed bandits who stole whatever they could, wherever they could. This included night time raids on the Firestone plantation during which the bandits tapped the trees and stole the latex, often in a manner that left the tree useless afterwards. Firestone's security guards were regularly attacked or killed while they tried to defend the property. In the meantime, I listened to a BBC radio program during which the interviewer asked a government employed school teacher in Liberia how much he earned. The reply was "Thirty dollars per month, but I haven't been paid for three months".

Other media reports accused Firestone of polluting a local river and rendering the water unusable. When I visited the river, I saw that there was some outflow to the river but I could also see people swimming, washing and fishing there. A few short miles away, the raw sewage from Monrovia city was seeping, untreated, into the river and the sea. These contextual comparisons were never made in the media reports and journalists continued to attack the corporation.

Firestone's commitment to Liberia was total. After my first visit, I returned to Europe feeling reassured. This was CSR in action. The financial investment being made in the unstable West African country carried a huge risk of low or no return. Building schools and hospitals for workers and their families was rare in West Africa. Despite several accusations of the use of child labour, the only children I saw were those travelling to and from schools where they were being educated by company-paid teachers. My visit gave me first-hand information and data about what was really happening in Liberia. When major customers contacted us for a response to the accusations in the media, I was able to reply with conviction and pride in the company's efforts.

One year later, I was invited to return to Liberia to see the progress that had been made. I accepted and was accompanied by colleagues from America and Japan. My Japanese colleague, Kawano, was the first person from Bridgestone Japan to visit the Liberian facility in ten years. No one in Japan wanted to be associated with it because the general consensus was that it was a dangerous place: both for the lives of those who went there and for the image of the company. The Japanese were therefore happy to leave it under the management of the American subsidiary who were all westerners. My own opinion was that the company was performing great CSR activities there, and this view was shared by the President of Liberia, Ellen Sirleaf Johnson who, in her speech at the re-opening of the Firestone-owned and managed hospital in Duside in December 2008, referred to the unfavourable media reports and said that people should not give an opinion on what was occurring on the plantation without first coming to see it for themselves.[21]

As a PR professional, I believed that we should have leveraged investment in Liberia to add credibility to our corporate values. In spite of my many efforts to explain this to my Japanese management, I never won their support. They did not want to raise the awareness of Bridgestone's presence in Liberia. Large corporations have great difficulty being consistent in their values and behaviour. While what was happening in West Africa was a great example of CSR in very difficult conditions, closer to home, in the relatively favourable conditions of the developed world, it was very difficult to implement even the simplest initiatives.

Getting the Corporate Philosophy Through to the Organisation

The gap between the vision of the global CEO and the actual situation in the subsidiaries was demonstrated when it was discovered that the

---

[21] http://firestonenaturalrubber.com/video/20081212_sirleaf/sir)leaf_pr.htm
(See the video at
http://firestonenaturalrubber.com/video/20081212_sirleaf/sirleaf_pr.htm)

Marine Hose Division of Bridgestone was a party to a cartel. Bridgestone was one of a small number of rubber companies that manufactured giant hoses used for loading and unloading bulk liquids like oil from ships. It turned out that Bridgestone (Japan), Dunlop Oil & Marine (UK), Parker ITR (Italy), Trelleborg (France), Manuli and Yokohama all had a well-organised cartel that would meet, fix prices and agree to tenders for business. The companies were found guilty in several jurisdictions including the USA and the European Union. Bridgestone was fined 58.5 million Euros under EU law alone. The total penalties across the world ran into more than 100 million Euros.

The European Commission has imposed a total of € 131 510 000 fines on five groups – Bridgestone, Dunlop Oil & Marine/Continental, Trelleborg, Parker ITR and Manuli – for participating in a cartel for marine hoses between 1986 and 2007 in violation of the ban on cartels and restrictive business practices in the EC Treaty (Article 81) and the EEA Agreement (Article 53). Yokohama also participated in the cartel but was not fined because it revealed the existence of the cartel to the Commission. Marine hoses are used to transport crude oil to and from ships for transportation from production sites. The cartel members fixed prices for marine hoses, allocated bids and markets and exchanged commercially sensitive information. The fines for Bridgestone and Parker ITR were increased by 30% because of their leadership of the cartel. Manuli was granted a 30% reduction of its fine for its cooperation with the investigation under the Commission's leniency programme. [22]

A high-ranking official in the European Commission Directorate of Competition, whom I knew, confirmed to me that it was recognised within the Commission that the top management of Bridgestone was probably completely unaware of the cartel, and that this was often the situation in similar cases. This was also my belief. I had reported directly to the global CEO for several years when the cartel was discovered, and I had complete faith in his ethical standards. In fact, as a result of the scandal, he decided that the company would withdraw from the marine hose business even though it had been very

---

[22] Europa press release Jan 2009.
http://europa.eu/rapid/pressReleasesAction.do?reference=IP/09/137&type=HTML

profitable. He was unwilling to continue with the business unit as a part of the group after it had disgraced the company. I admired his decision and I included the cartel story in my lectures to employees about ethics. I believed it was important that employees knew about the severity of his response and I hoped that they would consider it a benchmark against which to measure their own behaviour.

Earlier, I quoted a Meiji university study that suggested that CSR has become a fashion among Japanese companies. In this regard, it is interesting to look at the corporate philosophies of Japanese companies such as Olympus which, as we have said, was almost declared bankrupt,

In all our business operations, we strive to play an integral role in society, sharing its values and working to create new value to help people around the world have healthier and more fulfilling lives.

This is the essence of the Olympus management philosophy of Social IN. As a member of society, Olympus places the utmost importance on its relationships with individuals. Accordingly, Olympus has adopted Social IN, a management philosophy that embraces social values as an essential part of its business ideology.

Olympus was founded with the declared purpose of manufacturing microscopes that would garner recognition in the global market. The impetus for this drive was a deep sense of duty to help advance medical development through the domestic manufacture of microscopes.

Since then, Olympus confirmed its position as a camera manufacturer and developed gastro cameras. Following this achievement, Olympus made a number of dreams come true through the application of Opto-Digital Technology, an area of core competence that integrates longstanding optical technology and state-of-the-art digital technology.

"Your Vision, Our Future" embodies our determination to realize dreams in a close bond with society while coexisting in harmony. Based on this corporate slogan, Olympus is pursuing innovation in order to become a company where all stakeholders, including shareholders,

clients and employees, are proud of the Olympus brand. [23]

If the Meiji University study is right, then we can see that the "fashion" is catching on, and just like any fashion, the same materials and designs reappear.

Communication with Stakeholders

Another important responsibility for today's corporations is investor relations. Open and honest communication with investors or shareholders is expected and is identified as one of the corporate responsibility issues in Bridgestone. However, commitment to this principle turned out to be limited to the release of financial results and forecasts which, in any case, as with all large corporations, are available on the company's website. Most Bridgestone shares are held by Japanese institutional investors although they are traded and available to investors around the globe. The company issues a briefing to shareholders when the financial results are released in each period, but only in Japanese.

In the first decade after 2000, there was an increase in the number of companies and organisations that provide recommendations and advice on ethical and responsible investing. These organisations, many of which are located in Europe, prepare analysis of the corporation's activities based on studies and questionnaires that are sent to the companies under scrutiny. Bridgestone as a Fortune 500 company was often the subject of these studies. During the period of the global attention on Liberia, which was accompanied by reports of infringements of international labour and human rights by Firestone, attention focused on Bridgestone's ethical standards and behaviour. Questionnaires and/or queries were sent to Bridgestone's headquarters in Tokyo and were addressed to the chief executive officer. I learned about this when the company doing the study contacted my office for help because, in spite of all its efforts over several months, it had failed to get a response from Bridgestone headquarters in Tokyo.

I also discovered that there were no records of the enquiries being

---

[23] Olympus Corporate philosophyhttp://www.olympus-global.com/en/corc/profile/philosophy/

received at headquarters. If this had only happened once I could have believed that an administrative error had occurred, but it had happened every time. It was evident that Bridgestone was not recognising the authority of the organisations to undertake the analysis. The pressure we were feeling in Europe from customers, media, investors and others created levels of anxiety that simply were not understood in Japan where those in charge of investor relations knew that the majority of the shareholders were Japanese and that they were unaware of the reports in the Western media. The issue simply was not a priority for them. The end result was that because there was no response from Bridgestone, the corporation could not be recommended as an ethical investment.

This behaviour also underlined the attitude of the Japanese headquarters towards its European subsidiary. This was not the conduct of a truly multinational company. It was the attitude of a Japanese company with an overseas office. Even if the overseas office had 13,000 employees and a turnover in excess of three billion Euros, it was still just an overseas subsidiary and did not warrant the same care and attention as the home market or the home investors.

To underline the positive discrimination towards their home base or domestic market, the company took extraordinary steps to support the reconstruction efforts in north-eastern Japan following the 2011 earthquake and tsunami. A company policy was issued that gave precedence to the supply of products and services to the reconstruction effort over all export customers. While such a policy is understandable, it reinforces my understanding that Japanese companies, wherever they are located, are first and foremost Japanese. They pursue policies and activities that benefit the Japanese. A non-Japanese employee will need to understand this context and to accept this unwritten law of business practice within Japanese companies.

Chapter 8

Branding and Advertising

Understanding Consumer Behaviour

In an interview with CNN in June 2012, the very successful former CEO of Tesco, Terry Leahy, talked about business strategy. His simple recommendation was to start with what the customer wants and not what you have and to recognise that customer needs change and develop. A successful business will be one that understands changing needs and that responds effectively to them. My consumer research showed that European motorists prefer to buy their tyres from a local business and that they preferred that the service provider be close to where they live or work: they look for convenience. However, the message from the top executive offices of some Japanese companies is that consumers want or need a pan-European network of tyre shops that provide the same products with the same levels of service everywhere. They derive this belief from experience in their domestic market.

I understand how this concept works for a hamburger chain, but for a product which consumers buy in many cases only once in two or three years, it seems that a pan-European network is of no importance to them. Local companies that tailor their channels of distribution to meet the needs of the local market have a distinct advantage. The Japanese do not understand this. They believe that what works in Japan should work in Europe. It takes a long time to learn the intricacies of consumer behaviour that often differ from region to region. Non-European executives on short-term assignments in European settings cannot be expected to learn about, understand and adjust to the cultural differences between one part of Europe and another. It takes time to do this. More proof that the Japanese can be leaders in developing good products but that they have a long way to go in improving their marketing and consumer insights.

Nowhere was this clearer than in Bridgestone's approach to television advertising during its long association with Formula 1. Advertising cultures in Japan, the United States and Europe differ: one may use a subtle approach, another a more direct one depending on the purpose; some advertisements sell or promote a product or an offer, others are intended to enhance the image and perception of a brand. Participating in Formula 1 offered Bridgestone a coveted global platform. The core activity fitted well with the main products and the local activation could be tailored to local needs and conditions. Yet, corporate headquarters persisted in creating television advertisements for global distribution and failed to adapt their idiosyncratic style of television advertising to western or non-Japanese contexts. Over time, it was clear that Bridgestone simply could not understand the style and preferences of European television audiences and it had failed to take advantage of the global audience Formula 1 provided.

Using Formula 1 to Establish Brand Credentials

Entering the F1 world in 1997 was a huge step for the company; it offered a unique position in communication and brand development, and brought the brand name to a huge global audience. It was expensive but it was the right direction at that time and served the company well, especially in Europe. Within three years, the spontaneous brand awareness of Bridgestone had increased by around 20% in the major European markets, but after five years, this evolution started to level off and reached a saturation point. Several surveys confirmed this trend in spite of the high cost of sponsoring the sport.

The first years of Bridgestone's involvement with Formula 1 presented a golden opportunity for its marketing and promotional campaigns. Integrated materials and events were developed and included, among the most successful ever, the *Local Hero* campaign. Briefly explained, the campaign drew on the idea that each country had a Formula 1 driver who was adulated in his country. In 1999, Michael Schumacher was Germany's favourite, Jean Alesi, France's, David Coultard, the UK's and so on. We in Bridgestone Europe developed a range of point-of-sale materials that comprised life-size posters and cut-outs of the *Local Hero* with his testimonial support for Bridgestone tyres. Dealers were eager to have these materials and end consumers were buying them, even stealing them when they could. Such pull through demand enabled the sales forces to leverage orders from the dealers in return for the materials. But every campaign is finite, and after two years of this one, it was time to move on.

When I questioned the wisdom of continuing in Formula 1, I was told that no other activity could associate our brand with such a high-tech world, and that it underlined our tagline, *Passion for Excellence*. In 2011, I was one of several in the management team that favoured moving on from Formula 1 to another activity after the fourteen-year association. No substitute activity was agreed upon although several alternatives were discussed. Formula 1 had become part of the Bridgestone "institution" and it would be extremely difficult to end the partnership. Many people, especially those who had a strong personal interest in the sport, had made it a big part of their personal purpose in life to resist giving it up. When Bridgestone's top management finally took the decision to withdraw from the sport, there was a huge backlash from several key executives. In my opinion, Bridgestone's withdrawal came at least eight years later than it should have, but it should never have taken place before another activity had been chosen to replace it.

In retrospect, I realise that I should have kept my opinion to myself because my experience should have taught me that suggesting an idea that contradicted that of senior Japanese managers was potentially suicidal. Today, I believe that because I had expressed my support of withdrawal from the sport freely, I was excluded from the circle of management who were passionate followers of Formula 1 and that as a result, I was not going to survive in the company.

The Challenge of Changing Direction

When the corporation developed a new tagline for the brand, *Your journey, Our passion* the Tokyo headquarters issued a directive stating that, if necessary, it could be translated in parts of the world where English was not the business language but elsewhere the English version should be used. My team surveyed the European markets and discovered that some of them preferred to translate the new tagline into their local language. When I reported this to Shimbashi, my CEO and boss, he grew angry and accused me of creating unnecessary difficulties. He turned to the members of the executive management committee, the EMC, and asked its various Japanese members, and in particular Sakamato who had lived and worked in Germany, for his opinion. Sakamato knew the answer that Shimbashi wanted and like all the other Japanese, replied that the English version would be acceptable.

The only market that was not represented at the meeting was Italy. I was instructed to check with the managing director there. He happened to be Italian. Realising that he may not get the answer he wanted from the Italian, Shimbashi revised his instructions. I was not to check with the managing director of the sales company in Italy, but instead with Paulo, the managing director of the research centre, also in Italy. I knew why. Shimbashi knew Paulo's character well enough to know that he could trust him to give the "right" answer. When I contacted Paulo, he wanted to know why he was being asked the question. He admitted that he firmly believed that the tagline should be used in Italian, but asked me to give Shimbashi the answer he wanted. He considered that it was far more important to continue the charade than to do what he thought was right in the market. I reported Paulo's answer to Shimbashi; he beamed.

One Size Fits All

Shimbashi went on to suggest that our television advertisements should also be in English. His narrow view of Europe was that all educated people spoke English at least as a second language, and that Bridgestone could therefore save money by producing English versions only. The frustration that this created among the European marketing team needs no comment, but we had finally accepted that senior level Japanese managers always believed that they were right and we complied. We had understood that we would need to be patient in all our dealings with Japanese CEOs, whose dangerous blend of overconfidence and lack of knowledge of local marketing needs often characterised them. We were lucid enough to comprehend that non-Japanese employees who aspired to a career in this kind of environment would have to accept that they would often have to ignore their common sense, knowledge and experience if they were going to survive.

Once again, corporate headquarters created television advertisements for global distribution. In the early years, these were Japanese advertisements translated into English. Later, under pressure from the European marketing team, efforts were made to create advertisements that were more European in style, but they nevertheless remained disappointing. During this period, Bridgestone USA which was more than double the size of the European company and more profitable, broke away from the Japanese marketing model and created its own distinctive advertising and communication style. This was exactly what was needed. The American company developed a series of sports sponsorships and leveraged each to reach different audiences whether they were NFL, NHL or golf fans. The marketing team in Europe tried to emulate this approach with limited success. The first problem was that the only common European sports were football and tennis. The second was that decision-makers could not agree on which sports to sponsor. Some lobbied to limit support to Formula 1; others did not like tennis, others felt that it would be too expensive to sponsor European football. Finally, European investment in marketing depended on funds from Japanese headquarters and these funds came with an obligation to accept Japanese creative input, including Japanese advertising agencies. It was, therefore, a constant battle to infuse a European flavour into the concepts.

Frequent Change of Image

During my time with Bridgestone, the company slogan changed several times: *A Grip on the Future, Passion for Excellence,* and *Your Journey, Our Passion* were the three more recent ones. All were surprisingly similar to the slogans of other companies. This made it particularly difficult to differentiate one slogan from another and, therefore, one brand from another.

The slogan, *Passion for Excellence* was associated with the Formula 1 brand. When Bridgestone withdrew from the sport, top management wanted the slogan replaced. The branding experts in Bridgestone Americas and Bridgestone Europe advised against this arguing that *Passion for Excellence* could and should continue to be the company slogan and that there was a case for continuing with a well-established and recognisable catchphrase. A brand enhancement committee, made up of all Japanese members of the Board, was created in Japan and concluded that the withdrawal from Formula 1 should be complemented by a new direction and a new vision for the company.

They decided that henceforth the essence of the brand would be "supporting the lives of individuals" and the new slogan should be, *Your journey, Our passion*. The views of the non-Japanese were ignored but we were nevertheless charged with the task of communicating the new thinking.

From the very beginning of the Formula 1 years, I had always argued that the real return from the investment in the sport would come when we left it. We would drop the huge cost but we would gain from the "long tail effect" whereby millions of consumers would continue to associate our brand with the top motorsport in the world. This possibility was lost when the decision to break with the sport was coupled with the waiver of the slogan *Passion for Excellence*.

Even if we did not agree with the new direction, it would have been easier to accept if the company had invested in a new area after Formula 1. The marketing teams waited for the next big communication tool and hoped that it would be another sport which would provide a whole new audience. Regrettably, no project replaced Formula 1.

With the exception of the fourteen years in Formula 1, no consistent context in which to establish the Bridgestone brand was ever developed. This was, in part, due to the frequent changes of leadership: every new CEO had his own idea of how the brand should be promoted. This led to a regular cycle of change that disregarded what had gone before whether it had been effective or not. The paradox is that the domestic market in Japan boasts many consistent and long-term programs. So why then is the approach to brand development in Europe so different? The response is that marketing teams in Japan are neither adventurous nor willing to try anything abroad that is not consistent with their domestic strategies at home.

Japanese and European colleagues in the same company view their presence in the local markets differently. For example, my European colleagues and I believed that the company could promote itself more aggressively. The Japanese view was that because the company was an outsider in Europe, it was important to be as discreet as possible because negative publicity about the company's activities could filter back to Japan and damaging media coverage had to be avoided at all costs. The Japanese view almost always prevailed.

There is another lesson to be learned here: a westerner joining a corporation with headquarters outside Europe should consider very carefully how that corporation behaves in Europe. If decisions are systematically made at headquarters, it may mean that a local employee will only survive in the corporation if they do what they are told. Anyone wishing to build a career by applying their skills and knowledge must be prepared to simply follow instructions without challenging them even if this means that they must discount what their common sense tells them, what their knowledge exhorts and what their conscience dictates to be in the best interests of the company.

Give a Consumer What {S}He wants, Not what You Want Him/Her to Want.

The Bridgestone marketing team regularly implemented consumer surveys and focus group discussions about car owners' buying habits, their purchasing habits and their responses to tyre advertising. It became very clear that the majority of motorists hardly think about tyres at all. Their level of interest in tyre technology is low. Of course there are some motorists who are passionate about everything to do with their car, but they make up little more than 10% of the market.

At Bridgestone headquarters, the marketing and brand management department was run by the product engineering and development department. This meant that the decision-makers were engineers who were more interested in the technical features of the products than consumer views about those products. I identified this weakness early on in my time at headquarters. The technical experts prepared marketing materials which were packed with icons and buzz-words about the different technical features involved in the production of the tyres. Now, as then, it is difficult to imagine why a motorist would care that a tyre had been built using RCOT (Rolling Contour Optimisation Theory). The product specialists were very proud of these features but no-one else really understood what they were, not the salesmen and certainly not the end consumers. I tried to convince the company to turn to the marketing department rather than to the engineers for publicity and communications about the products. The technical input was an important part of the process, but the driving force behind advertising campaigns had to be the needs of the customer with whom we should communicate in language they understood.

My experience and my education had taught me to understand the difference between features and benefits. Features distinguish one product from another; benefits sell an idea to the consumer. We had engineers and developers who talked enthusiastically and knowledgably about the importance of tie bars or the silica content of tyres, and who would advocate for them as key selling points. I tried to explain that the average consumer was not interested in these features, and that we should focus on elements that mattered to them, including stability and wet grip which were security matters that the average consumer could understand. The engineers took as a personal insult my suggestion to ignore the technologies they extolled, and dismissed my suggestion as a short-sighted form of tunnel vision. I persevered and, using hard facts derived from expensive consumer research, I managed to convince the team that we should push benefits rather than features. We briefed advertising agencies and they prepared their proposals. Their arguments almost always emphasised the better braking performances and handling characteristics; benefits which would certainly appeal to motorists. But the final acceptance of all advertising proposals was made at the CEO level, and the CEO was always Japanese and habitually preconditioned to believe that the engineering and technical content was the most interesting feature in any advertising campaign. Once again, even though the survey results clearly showed that this view did not reflect the objective reality, the Japanese view dominated.

Consumer behaviour has shifted dramatically since the 1960s. I recently read a presentation called, *How to Advertise* in which three key pieces of advice are offered to companies. They are, Don't interrupt me-entertain me; Make it relevant, I want a dialogue not your monologue.[24]

Apart from being succinct, these principles have another encouraging quality – they assert the validity of my personal business mantra which has always been "tell the customer what they want to know, not what

---

[24] Personal Branding 2.0. David Merzel. Davidmerzel.wordpress.com

we want them to want." I am comforted to see outstanding professionals agreeing with my advice. To date, there is little evidence that my Japanese colleagues have either heeded this advice or that they will in the future.

Different Messages Appeal to Different People.

For some years, the Japan-based advertising department insisted in using Japanese-based media buying agencies to handle the media buying in Europe. The briefing was decided in Japan, and the plans were discussed and accepted there as well. Just before the contracts were signed, the proposals were shared with the European office but with no supporting explanation, and with only a short deadline for feedback. In other words, the input from the European office was not wanted; management wanted only to be able to say that they had shared the information with the Europeans before the final decision was made.

As a consequence, millions of Euros were spent badly. A proper analysis of the target audience had not been part of the project and television channels were chosen because of their geographic reach instead of their demographic reach. It took several years of diplomatic negotiation with the Japan-based team before the situation changed and European advertising initiatives became more effective. The last television advertisements with which I was directly involved were created primarily for the European market, and I have to say that the co-operation between the Japanese and European marketing teams was excellent. The two advertisements that we created won awards, and created social media conversations at a level we had never witnessed before. They were successful from a European advertising perspective. In spite of all this, the CEO in Europe at that time did not like them. The fact that we had tested them in focus groups and consumer panels was not important to him. The fact that they won awards was irrelevant. They just did not appeal to his taste. The evidence was clear that these advertisements were appropriate and effective for the European consumers, and yet Shimbashi was so confident in his own judgment and expertise in such matters, that he criticised me and the European marketing team for having created them.

I was again faced with a dilemma. Should I use my expertise, perform the relevant research and testing, appeal to my audience, or should I simply give the CEO what he wanted and what appealed to his taste? Former CEOs had sometimes accepted that there were differences between Japan and Europe and that these should be respected. However, others like Shimbashi and the sleeping Mori, had such a strong bias against local staff and an unmatched confidence in their own opinions that European management was often left with no choice but to yield to their wishes.

Several of the European management team suffered in this environment. I was one of them. Loyalty to the company was our driving force, and we found it very difficult to accept the subjective decisions of CEOs who would soon be moving on to another part of the world, and whose decisions would invariably be criticised or ignored by his successor.

Brand Development – a Playground for Top Executives.

Japanese brand names are linked to a high quality image. Japan had no less than six brands on Interbrand's "Best Global Brands 2010". They included Toyota, Honda, Canon, Sony, Nintendo, and Panasonic. Although Toyota's reputation was negatively affected by the spate of recalls that occurred in 2011, it continued to be valued as a high quality brand. Japanese tyre brands, of which Bridgestone is the largest, benefit by association even before any investment in brand promotion is made. Just as Chinese companies are struggling to lose their low-quality image, Japanese companies continue to benefit from an enduring perception of excellence. That may explain why the decisions of executives like Shimbashi and Mori do not have the sort of devastating effect on the brand that they might.

Sleeping Mori was convinced that he was a world authority on brand development. When he was awake, he would write up presentations about his suggestions about improving the brand image around the world. Under his leadership, Bridgestone introduced a pan-European children's drawing contest. It was actually a copy of a similar program that was run in the domestic market in Japan. The contest was publicised in schools in the neighbourhoods near our factories and sales offices. At its peak, it attracted only 56,000 entries across

Europe. The topic for the drawing was "How we will travel safely in the future". Mori believed that by associating safe mobility with our brand, and by appealing to children, we could reach two goals. We could reach the parents of the children who were our potential customers, and we would be developing the next generation of brand ambassadors. I had concerns about the numbers. The company invested almost one million Euros on the project, and that was even before costing in employee time. Reaching 56,000 children across Europe was a drop in the ocean and would have little impact on our brand awareness measurement. As well, it was very difficult to integrate the activity into our main sales promotion. Tyre dealers were not impressed.

Mori was nevertheless absorbed by his brilliant art contest. He decided that every child that entered the contest should receive a T-shirt with their own drawing printed on it. He insisted that the prize- giving ceremonies should be high-level events in art galleries. He thought that this would draw the attention of the media and give the company great publicity. Of course, the public relations department was blamed when few journalists showed up at any of the planned events anywhere in Europe. European subsidiary managers knew that their CEO in Brussels was expecting them to support the art contest, so most of them did, but privately, they complained that it was distracting from their team's efforts to do business.

I had learned that it was necessary to support the CEO's wishes even when I did not agree with them. I went along with the art contest, allocated the necessary resources, and made it happen. But then Mori went too far. At the time of the Paris Motor Show, a Japanese director who worked on my team showed me the instructions he had received from Mori. Four public buses in Paris were to be painted with drawings selected from the children's contest. The buses would run their normal routes for four weeks at an overall cost of 120,000 euros. I was furious. Although the money would have to come from my department's budget, I had not been consulted. The only reason I was being told about it was because my signature was required on the approval form. Under the circumstances, I felt I was justified in asking the CEO to explain his intention. He replied that when the public saw the buses in Paris they would be puzzled enough to want to investigate. They would learn that Bridgestone had sponsored the event and would learn about the company. I privately wondered if he was well and appealed to him to use only two buses instead of four to limit costs. He reluctantly agreed. I was present when Mori, beaming with pride, had his photograph taken in front of one of the buses. I still have to meet anyone who believes that the Paris bus investment had any value for the company and its brand development efforts.

This incident highlighted a fundamental difference between Japanese and European business cultures: European businesses that I know would have carefully discussed the project to ensure internal support before implementing it. As long as non-European companies blindly impose their ideas without getting the buy-in of the local teams, their progress will be slow and limited.

Mori demonstrated his branding theories and presented them to the European teams from time to time. In one of his lectures, he enthusiastically explained that a car stays connected with the road through four contact patches which are only the size of four postcards. This, he claimed, was proof that the innovative technology in a Bridgestone tyre was not fully understood and that we should emphasise this point whenever we could. My colleagues and I agreed that his information was interesting but we simply could not imagine how to use it to promote the brand. All tyres in Europe had similar properties and had passed European standards to be allowed on the market. Contact point with the road was an argument that would apply to all tyres whoever produced them. It might raise awareness about tyres, but it would not differentiate our brand from another, and therefore, would not help us to sell more. Besides, with the limited resources we had for advertising and promotion, I was convinced that we would be far more effective if we invested in promoting our brand and not tyres in general.

Mori did not appreciate my opinion on these matters. He would say, "You don't understand. We need to change people's minds to understand that buying tyres is an investment in safety, and not just a distress purchase". I understood his view and wanted to support it. However, research into consumer attitudes clearly showed that they never actually planned to buy tyres, and when they did, it was because the condition of their tyres was brought to their attention by their vehicle inspection or a near accident. Other research showed that the biggest influence on tyre choice was the garage or tyre centre making the sale, and that the two top consumer criteria were price and wet performance. Knowing this made it difficult to orientate our thinking about promoting the brand from Mori's idea about the four postcard size contact patches.

Another of Mori's favourite topics was customer care. He would often tell stories of cases where customer care excelled. One of them was about a colleague in America who was travelling to Japan on holiday with his wife and children. The first leg of the flight was from a major city in the United States to Anchorage, Alaska where the plane stopped to refuel. During this leg of the flight there was a meal service and the stewardess asked one of the children what he would like to eat. The eight year-old boy said that he would like a hamburger and fries but was disappointed to find that it was not available on the flight. A few hours later, after a short stop in Anchorage, the flight crew boarded the plane to continue the journey to Japan. The stewardess approached the boy holding a bag containing a MacDonald's hamburger and fries. The moral of the story was that superior service from the stewardess, and by association the airline, would guarantee that the family would never choose to fly with a different airline.

Everyone who listened to Mori's theories and stories smiled and agreed that it was possible to differentiate one company from another through excellent customer service. What we did not accept, and found sadly missing from his scheme, was any suggestion of how a tyre company could introduce customer service levels of a comparable nature.

Consistency or Change

Mori invested hundreds of thousands of Euros in a training program called 3C (Customer Care Culture) which never delivered anything and was abandoned the moment he left Europe. His successor, Kuruna recognised very quickly that the silo mentality was choking the company and introduced his theory of CFT (Cross functional teams). Many of the Europeans welcomed his attempt to break down the silos but later, when Kikuchi in turn replaced Kuruna, any mention of CFT was forbidden because the idea was dismissed as nothing more than basic business sense and unworthy of any special reference.

The series of changing European managers meant that policy and practice moved in a different direction with each new CEO. Since, as we have seen, Bridgestone Europe had eight CEOs over my fifteen-year period with the company, change was a constant. The lack of consistency in management policy was a huge impediment to Bridgestone's progress in Europe. It was also one of the most important sources of de-motivation among the local employees.

When Shinagawa was appointed the European CEO, he set a target of 50% unaided brand awareness in Europe to be achieved by 2007. Years later, when the company had still failed to come close to his unrealistic target, it became known as a symbolic target. Those of us with knowledge of how brand development in Europe works understood that in order to reach such an ambitious target the company would have to make a massive investment, one that the company could not afford. When we presented case studies of what other companies were doing, we were asked to develop initiatives that would be effective without engendering huge costs. The process became a playground for Japanese managers to launch projects whose success they knew full well they would never be held accountable for since they would have been transferred before anyone could measure the outcomes.

A frequent change of CEOs and top managers is often a fatal mistake for foreign companies working in Europe. Either the appointed managers should be in place for longer assignments, or power has to be delegated to high quality local staff.

The Web is a Western Concept

One of the areas that suffered greatly from the unhappy blend of constant change in leadership and Japanese conservatism was the company website. The communications department in the Tokyo headquarters was responsible for setting global guidelines for website development. In the first decade of the twenty first century, the use of the internet as a business tool was well-established and growing steadily in America and Europe. In Japan, the web was still largely seen as a tool to provide information that the company wanted to release, and not as a platform to provide access to what the customer or reader might actually be looking for. The result was that the information on Bridgestone's global website was factually correct but woefully uninspiring. Any idea of innovation in web communication was discouraged. A regular comment at global meetings was "we must be very careful with everything that appears on our websites, as they can be seen all over the world." As a consequence of this attitude, the European subsidiary struggled to convince management of the potential of the European websites.

From 1994 onward, the marketing and PR departments in Brussels struggled to convince top management to invest in the local website as a business tool. The European CEOs were unwilling to do so for two important reasons. First, they were conditioned by the conservative approach to the internet as a tool for communication in Japan. Second, they reasoned that any benefit that would be derived from the web presence could only be measured in the longer term by which time they would have moved on. There was an unclear line of responsibility for web activity. Was the website the domain of the IT department, the marketing department or the communication department? No-one knew and since there were valid arguments for each option, in the end the responsibility was shared amongst the three. The result was that there was no clear ownership, no clearly stated objectives and no commitment to developing something of value. This, in turn, meant that because each department had different priorities for the website, nothing happened.

Moreover, as the C suite filled with aging men, the generation gap between them and the internet generation became increasingly visible. With very few exceptions, managers who were in the last ten years of their careers had not adapted to the tools of the internet generation. They did not understand the potential of the internet and the tools that were evolving with it and did not, therefore, invest in them.

The brands of the future have measured the importance of the internet and social media as tools of communication. The trend is already firmly established in the Americas and is quickly spreading in Europe. If the Japanese and other Asian companies want to succeed in Europe they will have to shake off their conservative ideas and join the internet revolution. Using the internet merely to publish top line company information is not a business strategy. It merely ticks the box that reports, "Yes we have a company website." Fortunately for Bridgestone, the tyre industry, in general, is not at the cutting edge of internet use as a business tool. Nevertheless in 2010, Michelin launched an online chat room where consumers could ask Bibendum, their company mascot also known as the Michelin Man, any question related to tyres and get an answer from an expert online. Considering the diversity of languages in Europe, this was an innovative approach to internet use and displays a willingness to push boundaries and experiment in full public view. It is an approach that will never be taken by a Japanese company in Europe.

In their home market, the Japanese are prepared to talk to consumers, though not as yet online. The communications department in the domestic Japanese market has a call centre, staffed by seven operators, to handle complaints or take enquiries. Overseas operations were also encouraged to have a call centre that would handle customer complaints but the tools and systems that were developed in Japan for Japan were seldom rolled out to the operations overseas.

A Lesson in How to Confuse Your Brands

Meanwhile, the Japanese CEO in the overseas subsidiary was free to implement whatever brand development idea he wanted even when his training and area of expertise was from a non-marketing area. One of my favourite stories about how a top manager can impose his wishes against all expert advice is related to *On Track Signage* in Formula 1. Bridgestone signboards were visible all around the tracks. The well-situated signs filled the television screens of millions of people watching the races. The track organisers allowed a limited number of contracts at each venue, so there was little or no clutter and each participating brand would get good exposure. Names like Fosters, HSBC and Bridgestone shared the space and the brand exposure fuelled huge growth in awareness of the Bridgestone brand, especially in Europe.

On the top floor of the Bridgestone headquarters in Tokyo, Kato, the global CEO at the time, reviewed the reports and was pleased with the return on the company's investment in Formula 1. He wondered if there could also be a way to boost the brand awareness of the company's other global brand, Firestone. When Bridgestone took over Firestone in 1988, Firestone was huge in North America and was better-known in Europe than Bridgestone. As well, its market share in Europe was higher. Yet after the take-over, no investments were made in the Firestone brand and its visibility steadily declined.

Kato came up with what he believed was a brilliant idea: share the on-track signage at Formula 1 venues between Bridgestone and Firestone. For branding professionals like me and other colleagues, this was a foolish idea. We predicted risky confusion between the two brands by both end users and tyre dealers. At the time, the name of the company was Bridgestone Firestone Europe. Both brand names ended in the word "stone". Both brand logos were black and red. Both brands were involved in single-seat motor racing: Formula 1 for Bridgestone, and Indy car for Firestone. When I challenged the wisdom of the idea, I met resistance. My Japanese colleagues were quick to point out that to voice a challenge to the global CEO's proposal was comparable to treason. I tried to explain the logic of my argument, but the more I spoke the more resistant they became. In fact, they were shocked that I had dared to express such an opinion.

Although I firmly believed that I was right, I decided not to pursue my argument. Kato got his wish. The following Formula 1 season saw both Bridgestone and Firestone signboards displayed around tracks. On some tracks the signs were constructed in such a way that both brand logos were visible in the same television frame; on others, the signs appeared alternately so they read Bridgestone, Firestone, Bridgestone, Firestone. I was horrified at the inherent lack of understanding of brand differentiation. I was told to stop criticising the strategy and to accept that everywhere across the globe other branding experts were holding their peace and not challenging the global CEO.

It was nevertheless a high-profile mistake and its knock-on effects were fascinating to watch. Marketing people in several countries interpreted the strategy to mean that we could promote and overlap the two brands equally. Consequently, mixed promotional campaigns started to appear in different markets. Firestone was sold as Bridgestone at a lower price. Years of efforts to differentiate the two brands were wasted. After two years of displaying both logos side by side in front of a multimillion television viewership, a decision was taken in Japan to revert to the Bridgestone logo, and to remove the Firestone signs from the tracks. No-one ever announced why. No-one ever admitted that it had been a mistake. No-one would admit that Kato's idea had been wrong.

I learned another important lesson about Japanese business culture: no-one admits to making a mistake. In all my time at Bridgestone, I never heard a Japanese colleague admit that something had been wrong. In fact, on the few occasions when I proposed a change of direction because something was not working out, my suggestions were met with shock. An admission that something was wrong was too close to an admission of failure. I had grown up in a European business society where it was common to admit that something was not working and that it was necessary to take corrective measures, but this approach clearly contradicted Japanese business culture.

Forgetting the Positive Lessons from the Past

"In order to build a future, we must know the past."[25] I have always believed that we must learn from the successes and failures of the past and to build our future strategies with access to all possible accumulated knowledge and experience. At Bridgestone, the past was often ignored.

Before 1997, when Bridgestone entered Formula 1 as a tyre supplier and when I was still managing Bridgestone Ireland, the Bridgestone brand was hardly known in Europe, including Ireland. At the time, my annual budget for advertising and promotion was equivalent to a percentage of turnover, and as there was neither global nor pan European guidelines to follow, I was free to spend it as I saw fit. This freedom was a marketer's dream. Working together with a local public relations agency, I selected appropriate sponsorship, including *The Bridgestone Irish Food Guide* and local sports clubs, and created billboard and radio advertising to promote our selected dealer network. What we did was ground-breaking in the tyre industry at the time, and it resulted in a major increase in brand awareness and an increasingly loyal dealer base. In the meantime, the Bridgestone Europe organisation was being established but did not have enough

---

[25] Otto Frank (father of Anne Frank) 1970

resources to manage brand development across Europe. Therefore, in Ireland, we were able to continue our local strategy undisturbed, and even though our business represented only about 2% of the European business, it became very clear that the development of the brand was making real progress. It was one of the reasons that I was approached and invited to join the team in the European head office.

In the Japanese domestic market, Bridgestone was also doing a fantastic job. They launched effective advertising campaigns and signage programs; they sponsored different sports programs including the Bridgestone Open golf championship and other prestigious events. Anyone visiting Japan could not fail to notice or be touched by the Bridgestone brand in some form.

When I left Ireland for Brussels in 1997, Bridgestone entered Formula 1 and suddenly everything changed. For the first time, the company was making a huge investment in supporting the brand on a global level. Our marketing team welcomed this direction and prepared to leverage the activity. However, in order to finance the investment in Formula 1, advertising expenses were reduced in each of the subsidiary companies. In the early years of Formula 1, the return from the new publicity was so effective that the loss of other advertising revenue was not important, but as the years passed and Formula 1 involvement became less effective in increasing the brand awareness, the loss of the advertising budget at each subsidiary company was increasingly problematic. Some of the countries that had been very effective in building the brand in the early years were starved of funds and, as a result, stagnated.

The Role of PR in a Japanese Company

Maintaining a brand leader position with high brand awareness is a very different task from building a brand from a low-level of awareness in a market full of better known competitors. Public Relations can be something of a mystery for the Japanese. Some think it is a cheap form of advertising; others see it as a tool to protect the reputation of the company. CEO Mori wanted us to find PR activities that cost nothing but that would yield wide positive publicity. CEO Shimbashi explained that PR was the most effective way to build brand awareness. He believed that we should issue press releases every day, and that my department's role was to ensure that the releases were published. He complained that he never saw any in the newspapers. When I pointed out that he only read Japanese newspapers and that he was unable to read most European languages, he demanded a daily press report. The remarkable thing was that Shimbashi actually believed that his command of English was superior to mine and, in fact, everyone else's. He regularly insisted on rewriting the draft press releases, often making them unintelligible, and since most were going to be translated into other European languages, his work was more of a hindrance than anything else. He never understood that distributing press releases about topics that interested few people was simply a waste of time.

The reality is that most of my Japanese superiors were afraid of the media. Once, during the Frankfurt motor show, the global president and CEO, Suzuki, took part in a roundtable press briefing with selected journalists who had been screened to ensure that they would not be "difficult". Almost all the journalists were native English speakers and, although Suzuki himself was relatively fluent in English, he insisted that the questions and answers should be made through an interpreter.

Suzuki spoke in Japanese throughout the briefing which focused on Bridgestone's global strategy. He was followed by Shinagawa, who was the second most important board member in the organisation at the time. Having worked with Shinagawa for three years, I knew that his English was more than adequate for the press briefing. To my horror, he delivered a synopsis of our European investments in Japanese, and, once again, the interpreter was called into action. This process continued throughout the question and answer session. The journalists asked their questions in English; the translator translated them into Japanese; Suzuki and Shinagawa replied cautiously in Japanese, and the translator translated the answers into English. By the time the replies came back in English, the meaning of the questions had been lost and the journalists were as enlightened as they had been before they asked their questions. The only outcome of the briefing was to alienate the journalists who later asked me not to waste their time again with useless press briefings in the future.

After the session, I asked Shinagawa why he had not spoken in English.

My question embarrassed him. He explained that if he had spoken in English it would have presented Suzuki, his boss, in a bad light. It would have been disloyal for him to show that Suzuki was less proficient in English than he was. During my years in Public Relations, this thinking resulted in the team hosting many fewer press events than I would have liked or should have been expected from a company the size of Bridgestone.

It was common to hold a press conference during an international auto show, especially if a new product was being launched. We always tried to use a good English speaker to make the presentation. Depending on the topic, it could be the head of our research and development department, or me in my role of vice president of sales or, later, communications. The Japanese philosophy was that the presentation should be made by the most senior person available, regardless of whether their English was understandable or not. To suggest otherwise was considered an insult. So time after time, I had to live through presentations to the press at auto shows by Japanese executives who delivered speeches of which only half was understood. Of course, we tried to make up for this by including copies of the speeches in the press packs, but we always felt that we had failed to achieve the level of professionalism we aspired to. On one occasion, I brought the CEO's deputy to the press briefing of Toyota Motor Europe. The head of their public relations for Europe, a Belgian, made the presentation in perfect English. At the end of his briefing, he introduced the European CEO from Japan who had been standing slightly behind him. The photographers stepped up and took pictures of the CEO beside his company's latest car. The journalists were happy: they had their story and they had their pictures. It made no difference to them that it had not been the CEO who had made the presentation. The Japanese deputy to whom I was exposing Toyota's way, interpreted my contribution as offensive even though my intention had been to demonstrate how Bridgestone could be more effective with our press briefings. I wanted to use people's various talents in the most effective way, but my attempts were interpreted as unwelcome criticism of our top executives.

PR at Times of Crisis

The voluntary recall of millions of tyres in North America in August

2000 was probably the biggest crisis to hit the company during my years with Bridgestone. The company was totally unprepared to handle it. The tyres had mostly been fitted on Ford Explorers. They had been exported around the world and it was estimated that there were more than forty thousand in use in Europe. The crisis was widely reported in Europe's media and was a huge topic on discussion forums on the internet. It was impossible to avoid the topic. Yet, European top management first tried denial as a response: they announced that, "This is an issue for North America, not for Europe."

As the news spread, public concern grew and everyone wanted answers. Consumers around Europe who were using Firestone tyres tried to contact our company's offices in their local country to get answers, but since there were no help lines set up, callers invariably reached someone unprepared to deal with their questions. As for journalists, best PR practice suggests that in crisis situations four hours is the maximum amount of time one should take to respond to a journalist's questions and that, in many cases, one hour is the ceiling. In our case, getting approval for our responses was taking up to four or five days. The result was that journalists gathered their information from other sources and printed or reported their stories without our corroboration or comment. From the perspective of the public and the media, Bridgestone/Firestone was hiding behind a wall of silence.

When the senior management finally realised that the company was not organised to handle a crisis they decided to put someone in charge. That person was me, and the responsibility was in addition to my role as vice president of sales and marketing. Twenty-four hours a day was not nearly enough to handle both these responsibilities, but I nevertheless set about stemming the tide. We set up hotlines in all European countries and published the contact numbers on our website. We issued daily briefings to each office to be used in handling customer or media enquiries, and we started a government affairs contact program to keep the authorities informed of what we were doing. As for handling the media, I became Bridgestone's European spokesperson and did my best to handle media questions within difficult constraints.

It was my first taste of crisis management and I learned a great deal from it. For example, one of the key factors for success in my role was the ability to keep short communication routes and provide quick responses. Immediately after my appointment, I made contact with the European Commission to inform them about the steps we were taking to recall the tyres from the European market, and when the wave of media enquiries could no longer be ignored, I met with press and television journalists. My team and I had been forbidden to issue any statements without the approval from headquarters in Japan who, in turn transferred our queries to colleagues in the Nashville offices who were so mired in their own legal battles, they had no time to reply. I had several Public Relations professionals on my team and, together, we tried to explain the importance of replying to the media quickly and honestly. We also attempted in vain to describe why it was totally unrealistic to expect a journalist to wait four days for an answer. We showed how the journalists had kept to their own deadlines and had published their articles without our comments or inputs. The Japanese could not understand the speed of the journalistic world, and dismissed the journalists as rude because they had not waited for our answers.

I also learned that circumstances change rapidly and continue to change in a crisis situation. The Japanese approach takes too long and is already out of date even before it is completed. Just as the Japanese authorities played down the tragic Fukushima Daiichi nuclear disaster in 2011 and vacillated as the problems in the plant spread, so the Bridgestone leadership took too long to address the damage done by the recall crisis of 2000 and its consequences.

Another lesson derived from events that were taking place in North America. Nomura, the CEO of Bridgestone Americas was summoned to a congressional hearing where he was to be questioned about the fatalities that had resulted from the failure of the tyres.

Since Bridgestone had taken over Firestone twelve years before, the operations in the United States were run by a rotation of Japanese CEOs. Unfortunately for Nomura, he was in the seat when the voluntary recall was announced. American congressmen, who operate under congressional immunity, are free to make whatever comments they want during the hearings. They jumped on the opportunity to emblazon their image particularly those from areas where Ford plants were located. The hearings were held in public and filmed; the images were transmitted across the world. The workings of congressional hearings are well known by professional PR and legal advisors in the United States, and anyone summoned to appear before one is well-advised to prepare with the best PR consultancy possible. Did Nomura do that? We do not know. What we do know is that he appeared at the hearing and that the congressional committee lambasted him and castigated the company. In one of the most extraordinary displays of lack of cultural awareness I have ever witnessed, Nomura responded to their endless questions by adopting the Japanese cultural stance: he spread his hands in front of him, bowed repeatedly, and kept saying, "We are very sorry."

The congressmen had a field day. Unchallenged, they proceeded to play to their audience, and in the process damaged the image and reputation of Bridgestone. When the hearing was over, the reports were broadcast and Japanese management realised its mistake. There were several senior Americans in the management team whose advice had been ignored and whose help was now eagerly sought. One of them, Dave Lampe, replaced Nomura at subsequent hearings. He worked with lawyers and PR professionals before each hearing, and was well-prepared for all the attacks. He began the process of rebuilding the Bridgestone image and of limiting the damage to the company. He was rewarded by being appointed CEO of Bridgestone Americas. Nomura was sent back to Japan within two weeks and was retired from the company soon afterwards.

Bridgestone Americas was drowning in problems associated with the recall. In addition to the discussions with the congressional committee, they were dealing with an investigation by NHTSA (National Highway Traffic Safety Authority) which was threatening to force a wider recall. As well, there was a legal battle with Ford over who was at fault for the Ford Explorer accidents. The American team was working together to address these challenges but Mori, who was second in command in America at that time, believed that he could handle the situation better even if he did not understand the American legal processes. Without consulting the rest of the American management team, he made direct contact with people at Ford, believing that his man-to-man approach would lead to successful negotiations. He failed to understand that Ford was facing a multi-billion dollar lawsuit, and that the company was looking for any arguments to support its case. Mori unwittingly supplied the arguments they needed and, in the process, undermined the US management team's strategy.

The failure of both these Japanese executives to realise the cultural and legal issues at play as well as their inability to accept that they did not know what they needed to know to deal with the crisis, damaged the corporation enough to threaten its collapse. Following an ultimatum from the management team in the United States addressed to the head office in Tokyo, Mori was quickly pulled out and temporarily assigned to a back office job in Tokyo. Regrettably, a few years later, he was posted to Europe and became my boss.

Failure to understand cultural differences is potentially fatal for foreign companies operating overseas. We all suffer from prejudices and beliefs that condition our views; a company and its executives can only succeed if they accept this simple fact and take advice from well-informed, qualified local staff that can often see problems coming. I often illustrated this idea by using a story of two people standing on a railway track. One is European, the other Japanese. The European says to the Japanese;"I can hear a train coming we had better get off the track." The Japanese replies that he cannot see the train and that perhaps it is not coming. "Trust me," says the European, "I can feel the vibration in the tracks, and the train is getting closer." After a few more exchanges during which the Japanese explains that he has not seen enough evidence to support the idea that he should get off the tracks, the train hits him and knocks him down. When the train has passed, the Japanese sits up and says, "Ouch, we have been hit and injured by a train. We need to take a countermeasure."

The recall crisis continued for several months, but inevitably media attention moved on and we were able to begin to get the company back to normal. We did not ignore the lessons that had been learned and began to introduce a series of measures that we hoped would help us be prepared for any crisis that might occur in the future. We set up hotlines that were permanently staffed even though getting approval for the expense was more difficult than I had expected. We invested time and money to prepare a crisis communication manual with lists of contact names and numbers and other useful information to be accessed easily in the event of a crisis.

Beyond these minor programs, however, few of our suggestions were embraced. Our greatest challenge was to decide how Bridgestone would handle the media in the future. The recall crisis had taught us that, "silence is loud and clear." High-level journalists remarked that the company's unwillingness to comment on the crisis had been interpreted as an admission of guilt or fault. To help executives prepare for media questions, the Bridgestone Europe team organized annual media training during which a professional interviewer coached top executives and held "on camera" interviews to highlight areas of weakness. It became increasingly difficult to get our CEO to attend these training sessions. It was clear that the CEOs were reactive rather than proactive and that, in the absence of a crisis to deal with, the value of media training was dismissed. Today, in spite of all the lessons learned the Japanese answer to many questions remains, "We prefer not to comment."

The external public affairs specialists that had assisted us in the crisis communication work recommended that we organise a mock crisis day to test and train for preparedness. This technique is widely used in big companies in the west. On an appointed day, for example, a team of experts arrives at headquarters and announces a mock-crisis scenario. This could be, for example, an explosion and fire in one of the factories in which there have been injuries and fatalities, or it could be an industrial dispute that has led to violence. As the day progresses, circumstances change. For example, the team is informed that, as a result of a fire or an explosion, a leak of a dangerous chemical has resulted. The crisis management team must convene and handle the crisis and the communication about it. The experts play the role of television and newspaper journalists. The dynamics of dealing with a mock crisis like this quickly highlight the weak points of a company's crisis management procedures and, in the process, help to identify necessary improvements before a real crisis hits.

For six years, and under the management of three different CEOs, the Bridgestone Europe team planned and budgeted for a mock crisis day but every time, the day was cancelled. The top managers just did not want to do it because they simply did not see the need for it. For them, the recall crisis had become an unhappy memory and they preferred to forget it. The idea of preparing for a hypothetical crisis made no sense at all to them.

The reality is that in large companies crises and potential crises occur regularly. In 2009, the swine flu pandemic hit. Our CEO at the time, Kikuchi-san, had spent most of his career in research and development and was very methodical and process-oriented. As the flu pandemic evolved, Kikuchi predicted that if plants became infected, a serious drop in factory output could be expected. He decided to organise a meeting of the crisis management committee. The committee, which included most of the members of the executive management board, met every week to review various reports monitoring the health of our employees by location. Between meetings, the communications department was required to gather reports from all Bridgestone's main locations detailing the number of people on sick leave and what they were suffering from. While the process was challenged by some employees as an invasion of privacy, and probably not allowed under some national laws, it ensured that the threat of swine flu remained in the front of people's minds. My staff was asked to monitor various websites in Europe and prepare regular reports on how the pandemic was evolving. Kikuchi examined the trends and issued messages to all employees to keep them on high alert.

The installation of dispensers of sanitising gel and a programme of subsidised flu vaccines were among the preventative measures that were introduced. The only really difficult measure to implement was the obligation for employees to wear masks. In Japan, it is common behaviour for people to wear a mask over their mouth and nose when they have a cold or flu. In Europe, the local staff just could not get used to this idea; they considered it ineffective and strange. It is interesting that here again the cultural differences between the Japanese and the non-Japanese employees were highlighted. Blowing one's nose in public is frowned upon by the Japanese who prefer to snuffle behind their paper mask. Westerners found this behaviour bizarre.

As time went by, and as the World Health Organisation [WHO] neglected to update its website, it was clear that the threat from the swine flu had been over-estimated. As the risk diminished, information for our weekly reports was increasingly difficult to find. Finding the right time to officially end the swine flu crisis meetings became a new challenge. As long as there were reported cases of flu outbreak, it was argued that there was a risk that needed to be managed. Finally, in midsummer, the weekly meetings were abandoned.

Other crises occurred from time to time. Deaths and injuries in factories or negative reports in the media were regularly dealt with. However, the greatest crisis since the Second World War struck with the devastating earthquake and tsunami that battered Japan in 2011. Japanese people everywhere, not only those directly affected by the drama, justifiably felt personally implicated and were often plunged into deep crisis. In Bridgestone Europe, there were issues to be managed as a result of the disaster. Many of the tyres that were being sold in Europe were manufactured in Japan. There was no guarantee that supplies would continue to arrive. Raw materials for the plants which were imported from Japan were also in question. Some shipping companies suspended their services from ports on the east coast of Japan. The crisis management team began meeting three times each week. It handled the crisis very professionally and the experts in each sub-group not only managed their situations ably, they also reported thoroughly about them at each meeting. External communications, my team, was the only team that failed to meet expectations. In large part, this was because any replies to questions from journalists and other external stakeholders had to go through a rigorous process of control and consensus-building. All announcements had to get approval from both the European CEO and the departments in Japan that were implicated. The reality was that the company was unwilling to disclose any information whatsoever. This resulted in our team frequently replying, "No comment" and imparting only the most minimal and superficial responses. The same issues that we had experienced in the recall crisis of 2000 re-emerged: little or no respect for journalists' deadlines, and an unwillingness to communicate openly. More importantly, the inherent distrust of the non-Japanese prevents the Japanese hierarchy from conferring authority to local staff without internal approval. As well, their demand for internal consensus takes too long to meet both the very real deadlines to which western journalists are working and the norms of crisis communication. Finally, after the company's recovery from the recall crisis, executives in various positions continued to rotate. In the Tokyo headquarters, the key PR people who had lived through and learned so much from the crisis were replaced by younger inexperienced staff so that within a few years all the memory and experience drawn from the crisis was lost. The team in Europe managed to retain some of the experienced people and they tried to keep crisis preparedness on the agenda, but it was a losing battle. With every change of top management, the recall crisis moved further and further away from the company's centre of gravity. New appointees arrived with less and less insight and understanding about the importance of communication in times of crisis. And so, finally, very little changed.

Chapter 9

Conclusion

Up to this point, I have recounted real stories and incidents which I either witnessed or in which I was directly involved during my long career with Bridgestone. I chose them because I believe they illustrate both the challenges that Asian companies encounter in dealing with Europeans and which non-Japanese may confront when building a career in an Asian company. I have also referred to other books in which the author has described similar experiences and shared views about them that reflect my own.

In this final chapter, I will suggest how the future can be different. I will highlight how non-western and in particular Japanese companies can prepare a more positive business experience as they develop their presence globally. I will suggest skills and attitudes that western employees must acquire or improve if they want to succeed in the European subsidiary of an Asian company. Perhaps many of the same challenges exist in any mix of business cultures because difficulties in cross-cultural communication are not restricted to relations between East and West, or Japan and Europe, but I am limiting my considerations to my experience and the lessons I have drawn from it.

As I look to the future, I see a world where global communication will increase exponentially. International trade agreements are fuelling a growth in imports and exports globally, and an increasing number of corporations are becoming international or multinational. At the same time, the evolution of broad band and social media already supports, even promotes, global networking particularly among younger generations or "digital natives" for whom the online world has few boundaries.

The Need for Training

The evidence I have seen suggests that not enough investment or effort is made to support the internationalisation of Japanese business structures, and that efforts to increase the cultural diversity of Japanese corporations have been, at best, inadequate. I am aware that some organisations provide training and coaching in inter-cultural communication, but I fear that the need is far greater than these limited initiatives address. The starting point for any effective program of cross-cultural management is the fundamental acceptance that real problems exist and that these problems have a deleterious impact on business performance. Once this is established, top management must be committed to driving cultural transformation within the company.

When I look back at the number of Japanese staff and executives that were posted to European positions without any advance training, it is easy to understand why many of them struggled in their new environment. Conversely, I sympathise with the many Europeans who joined Bridgestone Europe with mistaken ideas about what it would be like to work in a Japanese company; too many either failed or were shocked by what they discovered. The human resources department developed different training tools, but they were generally designed to address skills and competencies in the workplace and seldom behaviours in a diverse cultural setting.

As I have already noted, in 1990, I was among a group of trainees from all over the world who travelled to Tokyo for training that was designed to develop insights into the mind and culture of the people we would be working with. We engaged in business and technical trainings. I am convinced that those two weeks of training prepared me to handle many of the difficult situations I confronted over the next twenty-two years, and that without that training, I might not have survived in the company as long as I did. Unfortunately, shortly after the program was over, the training of foreign employees in Japan by Bridgestone was stopped. High costs were used to justify the decision but it was also argued that because the company was more international than ever before, on-site training could be provided in overseas locations. However, my research has shown that at the same time that the training programs were rescinded, so also was the short-lived practice of employing non-Japanese in the Tokyo offices of Japanese multinationals. I am convinced that both these trends had a negative effect on cross-cultural understanding and consequently on the ability of Japanese and non-Japanese to work effectively.

Some years later, Bridgestone Europe developed a training centre in Rome, but none of the modules explicitly addressed cultural diversity.

154

Furthermore, none of the trainers were Japanese, so there was absolutely no opportunity for trainees to encounter, even tangentially, elements of the Japanese culture. There was probably no deliberate management decision to exclude training in cultural diversity; they simply focused on hard business and technical aspects because the field engineering department, and not human resources, supervised the training centre. The approach was wrong. As someone with first-hand experience of training in Japan and of managing staff members who struggled in a new culture, I knew that any costs that were saved by suspending the excellent training in Japan, were more than squandered by the high staff turnover and incessant conflicts that resulted because people who were forced to work together simply could not understand each other.

While I advocate for the training to be reintroduced, I understand that in a company with more than 130,000 employees globally there is a limit to the number that can be involved. Therefore, I support the principle that relevant programs should be developed and delivered closer to the local markets. This is simply a question of form. What must be accepted is that training in cultural diversity is imperative and that the elements of that training must include a thorough examination of what exactly cultural diversity constitutes; discussion and recognition of fundamental cultural differences; respect for cultural differences, and conflict resolution in culturally diverse environments. Such a program would bring measurable results in staff retention and would raise the profile of a company as a potential employer.

The Japanese executives who are selected for overseas postings also need extensive training and preparation. Of course the challenge for them is even greater because they are not just going to "the West", they are going to Spain or Germany or Dubai or Nashville and the cultural issues will be as different as their destinations. No executive is ever chosen for an ability to transcend cultural divides. Availability is usually the main criteria, followed by the demonstration of particular strength in disciplines such as finance or engineering. Executives are sent where those skills are needed.

Some of my Japanese colleagues told me about the two-day training sessions that they were given before being sent overseas. One of the key lessons was that they should never accept what they were told by a foreigner to be true. They were told that they should always verify the facts for themselves. A more positive approach would have been to highlight strategies and offer insights into ways by which they could improve communication and build trust. Training of Japanese executives must begin with the principle that non-Japanese employees with whom they will work also have qualities and knowledge that can be useful. If they can overcome the belief that the Japanese brain is superior to the western brain, then there is a chance that they can move on to deal with the real differences.

Managing Diversity and Fairness

A real respect for diversity infers equality both in the treatment and career opportunities that are available to employees regardless of their nationality or gender. Building a team of members whose individual contributions are equally valued would be far more effective in the 21st century than the military-style hierarchy in which Japanese members are more equal than the non-Japanese ones. I was surrounded by people who talked about teams but acted like sergeant majors.

For many years in my private life, I was a competitive participant in team games. I adhered to the idea that a strong and effective team is built on a foundation of trust, and I understood that success often crowned a team whose members believed in "everyone for everyone else". But I have also been a member of a team where one or two players, in spite of their superior skills, were too individualistic. These people undermined the team spirit to the extent that they damaged the overall performance of the team. Hence, the importance of looking for real team players. In his book, *Working for the Japanese*, Joseph J. Fucini describes the selection process that Mazda used in the mid-80s as they were looking for hourly paid workers for their manufacturing plant in North America: "Applicants were put through rigorous psychological role playing exercises and problem solving sessions. Mazda wanted people who could become part of a team." The Japanese business managers that I worked with subordinated the importance of team work to the supremacy of the chain of command. Soft skills were good to have, but only hard skills were measured. On the job training became the norm and, as a result, many local appointments failed.

If Japanese or any other eastern corporations are to prosper in the West, they need to look again at their team structures and build a real team spirit. Since the 80s the expectations of workers in the West have also changed. They expect, and are entitled to, more respect, training and recognition. They want to be valued. They cannot accept a "do as I say, not as I do" leadership. They do not accept this thinking on the sports field, and they will not accept it in the work environment either.

In 2011, the German automotive supplier, Continental published four new guiding principles. They were:

Passion to Win.
For one another.
Trust.
Freedom to Act.

These values would not be out of place in a top-level sports team, but they are equally valid for a corporation in the 21st century. They capture the essence of team work, and are a very attractive proposition for a potential employee. Compare these values with *The Bridgestone Essence* which was also published in 2011:
Integrity and Teamwork.
Creative Pioneering.
Decision-Making based on verified, on-site observations.
Decisive action after thorough planning.

Team values of trust and supporting one another are present in the values of Continental but absent from Bridgestone's. Bridgestone insists on verifiable facts through on-site observation, and testifies to a culture with an underlying lack of trust where, consequently, decisions are made by a very few who verify everything. I cannot believe that a large corporation with this philosophy can actually function successfully and be competitive in the 21st century. Perhaps a study of how the values and philosophies of corporations have evolved over the past thirty years is a topic for another book. Have the philosophies of Japanese corporations lost touch with industrial evolution? What can we expect from corporations emerging from BRIC countries? Will the values and management styles of Chinese companies be more like the Japanese or the Western economies? Today, I have no experience of working with companies from the BRIC countries, but I am sure that if they are to succeed in the West they need to address cultural diversity more seriously than the Japanese corporations are doing today.

What of the westerners who are working in a Japanese company in the West today or who are considering taking up a challenge in one of them? I am convinced that not everyone can survive or be fulfilled in this context, but for the person with the right attitude, background and expectations it can be a fascinating career choice. For women, provided they harbour no ambitions of climbing beyond a middle management position, it can be a great training ground. One female ex-colleague stayed in the company for eight years before Nimbashi, the woman-hater, dismissed her. She returned to her native Sweden, and now says that her on the job training at Bridgestone gave her a foundation and way of working that is appreciated by her present employers. Her attention to details, to facts and proper processes are highly valued, even if she was not appreciated by Nimbashi.

All westerners who choose a career in a Japanese company must accept that the Japanese are in charge. No matter what level of Japanese colleague you are dealing with, he or she is a part of a network from which you will always be excluded and into which you can never integrate. During my career in Bridgestone, I successfully negotiated and closed a deal which would subsequently generate a net gain for the company of 600 million Euros. To put this in context, the manufacturing and sales of tyres in Europe over a ten-year period did not reach a profit of 600 million. My contribution was acknowledged by the global CEO, but I never received as much as a 1cent reward or bonus for my efforts. Nevertheless, I felt that my efforts and contribution had earned me acceptance as a true member of the Bridgestone family. I believed that I was finally one of them. I could not have been more wrong. Over the years, as the management changed, any memory of my involvement in the original deal was lost. Each time new Japanese top management arrived in Europe, my standing in the company was reset and I had to earn whatever respect I could through renewed efforts. Most of my European colleagues faced the same challenge. We recognised the existence of a glass ceiling; a level beyond which it was not possible for a non-Japanese to go. In my early years in the European headquarters, I was promoted several times over a short period, but then I hit it.

The Japanese recognised that the limit to non-Japanese advancement was demoralising for the Europeans, so they made an effort to put some Europeans into senior positions, but these people were usually selected on the basis of their old age and their propensity to obey. Only Europeans that would blindly follow every direction without query were considered; all major decisions remained the monopoly of the Japanese; few, if any Europeans younger than sixty years old were promoted to high positions. In this way appointments could only last for two or three years. Yet even with these criteria, few non-Japanese broke through the glass ceiling and many world class managers with great leadership potential became frustrated and left the company because they were either too young or because they challenged business directions with good reason. A young visionary entrepreneur will be choked in this type of environment. Only hard-working, intelligent and respectful non-Japanese who are content to follow other people's directions without challenging them can hope to make progress, and even then, they will never have any control, even if it might look as if they do.

The management of the careers of the Japanese employees is different. From the outset, the corporate human resources machine follows and evaluates their progress. Even if their immediate superior is transferred to the other side of the world, their career development remains under the control of another authority. Meanwhile, the non-Japanese are evaluated by their immediate superior "N" as well as his or her superior "N+1". There are several performance evaluation programmes on the market. Bridgestone Europe adopted the PPDP system which required each employee to set a list of objectives at the beginning of each year which would be appraised by N at the end of the year. Personal development plans, linked to each individual's core competences and skills, as well as the required competences of the job were also included. In theory, the system looked very good and certainly ticked all the boxes in the event of an audit, but in practice it relied too heavily on the competence of each N.

One critical fault was that the Japanese staff members were unwilling to fill out their own objectives and achievements. They believed, probably correctly, that their performance and career management was being handled at the Tokyo head office. The additional burden of preparing objectives to discuss with a European boss did not fit with their perception of their position. They never openly refused to go through the process; they just would not do it. At one time when I had four Japanese direct reports, I challenged them for not having prepared their objectives by the due date. Each of them argued that they were so busy with other priorities, that they could not find the time to do it. They could easily list important business issues that had to be dealt with and point out that they were already staying in the office until 9 or 10 o'clock in the evening. They promised to attend to the task as soon as they had time. Of course, this "time" never came.

It was clear that the top Japanese management was on the side of the Japanese employees. Although they would never say it, they did not feel that the PPDP was for the Japanese. For most of the years that other Europeans and I were reporting directly to the Japanese CEO, we prepared our PPDP reports and sent them to our "N" who happened to be the CEO. The meeting and evaluation discussion which was the next step in the process never took place.

As long as a foreign company openly treats its home employees differently from its local employees it will be impossible to build a real team. In my example, my four direct Japanese reports could openly defy my attempts to include them into the same process as my other direct reports, and yet my European colleagues and I had no recourse when the process was applied to us. Further down the ranks, the system worked reasonably well. Even my direct reports were managing their own teams according to the policy, but they would not apply it to themselves.

Another open difference between the treatment of Japanese expats and all other employees was health care. Understandably, the Japanese were under the welfare and care of their home base. Their families underwent full health checks once every year at specially designated medical centres. The non-Japanese had no health checks organised by the company. Of course, all the employees had access to doctors and had medical insurance provided, just like every other Belgian resident, but it was nevertheless a two-tiered system which resulted in the non-Japanese staff feeling that the company cared more about the health and well-being of the Japanese staff.

My father worked for Exxon for most of his career. Exxon had a company doctor who provided annual medical checkups for all members of staff regardless of their nationality or origin. Such practice is common among big corporations. By choosing not to offer it at Bridgestone, the company created another factor that separated the Japanese from the non-Japanese and, in so doing, built walls between the different groups and fostered an environment that did not encourage team spirit. I am convinced that respecting diversity means eliminating these differentiating factors.

Integration

It would be unreasonable to expect employees of any nationality to adopt the culture of the country to which they are posted. It is perfectly acceptable that people on a foreign posting retain a preference for their own food, music, religion and hobbies. A clear respect for those preferences should be accepted and embraced by the host as well as the visitor. The problems that need to be addressed are related to the work habits, fairness and equality in the work environment.

Before coming to the European headquarters in Belgium, I had been used to being autonomous. While I did not have my own business, I had an entrepreneurial approach where I used my initiative to achieve the set goals. It was the combination of having the freedom to act and react together with my entrepreneurial attitude that fuelled the success of Bridgestone's business in Ireland. In fact it was the success of that business that identified me as a person they should bring to the European headquarters.

The difference in working environment between the small subsidiary and the big headquarters was beyond everything I imagined. I am convinced that the military-style structure crushed initiative and independent thinking. Not only I, but several of my colleagues had experiences where an idea or project which they were developing was blocked by their superior because it was not something they had been asked to do. Their boss would not have time to listen to the concept and background to the initiative, and killed it. Sometimes the initiator of the idea believed in it so strongly that they would persist over several weeks and try to get their idea understood or at least listened to. With very few exceptions, the resistance from the Japanese would finally kill the idea. The Japanese bosses were following directions from a higher authority - ultimately global headquarters. Logically, an independent idea from a local employee would not necessarily be in line with the Japanese directives. The local employee may have developed his or her idea based on the actual real market experiences or business environment. It may even have been in response to a movement of a competitor, but the management structure did not allow for independent thinking and use of initiative. Many good initiatives were lost, and many entrepreneurial spirits were crushed. Because these losses could never be measured, they were never acknowledged by the Japanese hierarchy.

Yet, inside Japan, especially in research and development departments, local Japanese were encouraged to use their creative thinking to develop new ideas. This is reflected in one of Bridgestone's four foundations *Shinshu-Dokuso = Creative Pioneering*. It is difficult to understand how this foundation is lost when the company moves overseas except when we consider the basic Japanese distrust of foreigners. Another theory is that the *Creative Pioneering* foundation only exists in the research and development activities, and does not spread to other departments. My experience tells me that there is truth in both theories, but that the fundamental lack of trust of foreigners is at the core of many of the problems.

Is it possible to change the attitudes of a cohesive group? Can people be taught to develop trust? One of my inspirations during my life has been the work of Nelson Mandela who built the trust of the different cultures within South Africa to a level where they could live together. I know the job is not finished and there are several obstacles still to be overcome, but when I consider the profound challenges that South Africa overcame in three decades, it becomes clear that with the right leadership many apparently insurmountable problems can be dealt with. The best example of this leadership that I ever saw was featured in the film *Invictus* which focused on the rugby World Cup which South Africa hosted, organised successfully on a global stage, and won in 1995.

Early in the film, we see a meeting of a sports administration whose members are newly-appointed black South Africans. The meeting votes to end the use of the name *Springboks* for South African representative teams because it is too deeply associated with the dominance of whites in the South African teams of the past. Nelson Mandela, played by Morgan Freeman, enters the meeting and gives a passionate speech about why it is wrong to take away those values that mean so much to the white population in South Africa. Instead, he wants them to keep the name and transform it into a name of which all South Africans can be proud regardless of their race or colour. This act of promoting peace and harmony through respect and trust is rewarded with the pride of the nation when the South African *Springboks* team lifts high the World Cup trophy.

Mandela's empathy is the kind of leadership that is needed to bring different cultures together in pursuit of a common goal. His vision is needed among members in the boardrooms in Japan, and steps need to be taken to cascade the philosophy throughout the organisation. It means changing long-held beliefs, but it has been proven that these changes can happen with each new generation. I look at South Africa, and I look at Northern Ireland where everything is far from perfect, but huge progress has allowed different cultures to work effectively together and build trust.

On my many visits to Japan I saw a different Bridgestone from that which I experienced in Europe. Many of the corporate social responsibility values that are referred to in their company reports and CEO messages are visible. Meals are provided at competitive rates, in-house travel agencies help employees with their private travel arrangements as well as their business trips, and there are several social activities organised by the company. There are even shops in each office facility where employees can buy the latest Bridgestone sports equipment and clothes, with special employee discounts. This consideration is rare for overseas employees. I know that Bridgestone's approach is that they should be competitive in employee benefits in each country or market where they are present. As a basic stance, that is perfectly logical and probably correct. In reality though, when local conditions differ substantially from what is done in Japan, then the Japanese model is not introduced because it creates too many additional costs.

Attitudes to Social Media

In the second decade of the 21st century, social media has become one of the biggest growth areas in the world. In North America, and soon after in Europe, the explosion of Facebook's popularity made it the platform of choice for social networking. Twitter and other tools also became important networking and communication tools. All over Europe, companies recognised the potential of these networks to promote communication at many levels, and even as a platform on which to advertise.

The policy inside Bridgestone Europe was that employees could not have access to social networking sites because there was a fear that some employees might abuse it and spend too much working time on their personal networking. As social networking evolved, the case was made to the top management that it should revise company policy. It was rejected. In the communications group, there were huge opportunities to use these platforms both in internal and external communications, while among prospective employees access to social media was almost becoming an expectation - much like access to a telephone or the internet. After months of frustrated debate, the real reason that Bridgestone blocked social networking was made clear: in Japan, employees were not allowed access to social networks. The fact that social network sites are not nearly as popular in Japan as in Europe was not even thought about. The fact that most competitor companies were not only allowing access to their employees but were also using social media as a communication tool was also not considered. It was simply a case of "we don't do it in Japan, so we are not doing it here". This approach was clearly in conflict with the idea of adopting local practices in employee benefits. It was another contributing factor to unhappy employees and high staff turnover.

In the late 90s, when the company was building its first website, there had been similar discussion about access to the internet. At that time, employees were not granted access to the internet from their office computers. After a long period of lobbying, the management reluctantly granted access to employees in Europe. I did not know it at the time, but access was granted only after it was agreed that employees in Japan should have access.

In late 2011, I attended a dinner of executive management board members to mark the departure of a Japanese CEO from Europe. During the dinner, the discussion turned to the topic of social media. The incumbent CEO proudly told the others that he did not even know how or where to find Facebook. One or two of those present admitted to having set up a Facebook account but were not regular users, while most of the Board members had never even seen it. It is important to point out that most of those present were Japanese, although there were a few older Europeans present in the group. I reflected on how conservative and out of touch this management group was.

To be able to lead a company with thousands of Generation Y employees, the management structure needs to be conversant with the latest social trends, especially when they are as far-reaching and important as the social media explosion of the 21st century. Non-European companies must recognise the trends and evolutions in Europe quickly if they are to succeed in their business and in recruiting and retaining employees.

The most recognised global employer for employee benefits and modern ways of working is probably Google, which regularly wins Best Employer surveys. They try to be the groundbreakers in managing employees as well as in the products and services they sell. The following quote is from Eric Schmidt, Executive Chairman at Google:

"The goal is to strip away everything that gets in our employees' way. We provide a standard package of fringe benefits, but on top of that are first-class dining facilities, gyms, laundry rooms, massage rooms, haircuts, carwashes, dry cleaning, commuting buses – just about anything a hardworking employee might want. Let's face it: programmers want to program, they don't want to do their laundry. So we make it easy for them to do both."

Google rolled out this philosophy across the globe as they established their overseas offices. I am sure that they also respect the local rights and expectations of their employees, but how refreshing it is to see a company not bogged down in tradition and conservatism. Which approach will fuel the successful companies of the future?

Promoting Employee Engagement

Today there are several business management books that explain how motivating employees and fostering trust and loyalty are among the keys to successful management. The relationship between a boss and his employee cannot be underestimated in this process. Open dialogue between the two can lead to a common understanding of expectations, which is critical for success. Yet, this is probably the one area in which I saw the biggest failures. Japanese managers felt that they understood their objectives, which in most cases had been set for them through links to the network in Japan, but they were often incapable of communicating these objectives clearly to their local employees. In some cases, the gruff or unapproachable manner of the managers made it difficult or even impossible for team members to ask for clarification and this led to unnecessary and damaging confusion.

Twice each year, the CEO would make high-level presentations about the company objectives to higher level employees. The presentation was charged with exhaustive lists of numerical data but included very few words to clarify the key points. It was humanly impossible to absorb all the information that appeared on each slide, and the audience was left with the impression that they were engaging in something highly confidential and that, therefore, there could be no questions or discussion afterwards. This was a one-way communication. The heads of departments, who had attended the presentations, were free to share the key points with their own teams but, when they did, it was inevitable that some of the focus and accuracy of the information was lost. As information moves away from its source, and if, on top of this, that information is being communicated in a language that is not clear either because people do not speak the language well or because it is opaque, misinterpretations are inevitable. And if no discussion is allowed or if no dialogue is generated, then it is very likely that few people will truly understand what the common goals are because the original message is actually not getting through. In spite of this, Japanese managers insisted that because the information was cascading down through the different levels, the information was being shared successfully so that everyone had received and understood the message. The result was, very often, a complete misunderstanding of company objectives which, in turn, triggered different levels of expectation and a mismatch of key performance indicators. This is bad management at its best.

What I never really learned was whether or not this was also the practice in Japan. However, as they are neither faced with the language difficulties there, nor with the mechanisms of mistrust that operate in the overseas subsidiaries, it is unlikely that the same problems exist. The great success of Japanese corporations in the last century could not have been possible without good management practice, which includes clear dialogue. I am therefore convinced that it is feasible for Japanese companies to succeed in the West if they manage cultural diversity better, introduce a culture of open dialogue and deal with their non-Japanese colleagues with trust and professionalism.

In the first half of the 21st century, we will see ever-greater investment from Asian corporations in Europe. Asian companies who are rapidly building their manufacturing and development capabilities all want a share of the European market, the biggest consumer market in the world. They will have to build organisations to run their business divisions in Europe, and they will have to employ Europeans to work with them.

The cultural habits of the Chinese, Koreans, and Japanese are quite different from each other. However, the way that they interact with, use, and treat their European teams will require similar understandings and approaches. It is possible to prepare for their European ventures more effectively than what I have seen from the Japanese to date. Many training and coaching resources already exist and can be used; what I am less sure about is how to eliminate the cultural prejudices that exist. Xenophobic mindsets, which already exist to some degree amongst European nations, are amplified between East and West.

Living in Brussels, the effect of the European institutions on the lives of its citizens is obvious. Increasingly, European university students are spending a year participating in an Erasmus exchange with another university in Europe, and it is refreshing to see the quality and international perspective of today's graduates. But this has taken decades to achieve, and there is still an older generation in the work force that has not benefitted from the same education. Japanese corporations, like Bridgestone, select graduates from a short list of top universities in Japan each year. Only rarely do they recruit employees who do not attend the institutions on this list, so many of the new hires have been educated in the same values and thinking processes. The high-potential recruits amongst the new intake are identified early in their careers and developed on a fast track. For the thousands of others, including most of the foreign overseas recruits, the career limitations are already stacked against them and they are consigned to a life of autocracy and bureaucracy. There are very few westerners who accept such a conformist regime. They inevitably become de-motivated which is neither good for them nor for their employer.

Modern education in the West fosters critical thinking. Gone are the days when students just read and retain other people's work. The graduates of today are well-prepared to add value and new thinking to the places in which they work. To benefit from human potential, an organisation has to provide an environment that allows freedom to act as well as continuous education and training. The successful companies of the future will be those where the human capital is nurtured and encouraged. This is far from what I experienced in a Japanese subsidary in Europe.

Preparing and Motivating Teams

Many of the mismanagement characteristics that I have described in this book are also evident in western companies with no Asian connection. Arrogance, bullying, inability or unwillingness to communicate, misuse of key performance indicators and other bad practice are found in companies all over the world. Management teams have to deal with all these problems if the organisation is going to survive and prosper. Foreign companies operating in the West have an additional challenge: they have to bridge the cultural divide and do all that can be done to avoid possible misunderstandings that can impact on performance. Just as I gained much from my training with the Japanese in my early career, others would benefit from similar cross-cultural training. Both sides of any cultural divide need to understand each other if there is to be any hope of building bridges. Respect and trust are also critically important and have to be earned but, if change is to happen, top management needs to encourage and support a culture of trust and respect. The current perception that foreigners cannot be trusted has to be changed. Otherwise high quality foreign employees will not be retained and only those that are unable to find employment elsewhere will stay with the company.

Teamwork, which is so often an assumed behaviour in the workplace, is regularly undermined by individualism, political ambition, or dictatorial leadership. Strong leadership is not all that is required to create an effective team; a common and shared understanding of the goals of each individual in the team and the team itself is also necessary. This kind of leadership can only happen when there is regular and thorough two way communication between the leader and the team members. Therefore, the ability of the team members to communicate with each other is critical. It follows that introducing team leaders with inadequate language skills leads inexorably to the failure of the whole team, even if the team leader has other excellent business skills.

After thirty years of trying to build bridges across the cultural divide, I recognise that it will take many more generations before companies from the East can flourish in the West. The Japanese have brought some excellent products and technology to the West over the past forty years, but excellent products and manufacturing practices alone are not enough to guarantee success. They have to be able to present them to the market and manage their operations in the foreign countries. Applying only Japanese marketing and communications styles, because that is what the Japanese management is comfortable with, will not be enough in the new business environments. Adapting to the needs of foreign customers and integrating the competencies of all employees are the first essential steps in the journey.

Acknowledgements

I am privileged to have worked with people of so many nationalities and to have had so much contact with others. Learning about different cultural behaviour has been a career long fascination for me.

During my time in Bridgestone Europe I forged friendships with some of my Japanese colleagues. Some of them took me under their wing and coached me, explaining the seemingly unexplainable. Without their support I could not have survived some of the situations in which I found myself. I will treasure their friendship always and I will spare their embarrassment by not mentioning their real names here.

In taking on this challenge to put my experiences on paper I was encouraged and helped by several friends and colleagues. Niall Murtagh an expert on Japanese relationships and author of The Blue-eyed Salaryman discussed my ideas in depth. Gerry McHugh advised me on structure, and my editor Katie Basha gave me hours of her time and patience. Ideas for the title flowed from Peter Collins and Agnes Foster. Suggestions of stories for inclusion and reminders of actual situations flowed from so many of my ex colleagues. I hope I haven't disappointed them with the final result.

Cultural differences lead to conflict and misunderstanding between Asians and Europeans. Nowhere is this more evident than in the overseas subsidiary of a Japanese Corporation. In Sushi and Fries the author illustrates the difficulties faced by European employees when working in a Japanese company. He also deals with the obstacles that Japanese managers face when they are assigned to Europe.

Using real life stories from his 30 years experience working for a Japanese Corporation in Europe, he shares his experiences some of which are funny, some tragic, but all are honest examples of what happens behind the doors of Bridgestone, a Fortune 500 corporation with its roots firmly in Asia.

The author was one of very few Europeans that reached the position of Vice President. From his vantage point he observed conflicts and confusion which regularly blocked business development and choked creativity and inspiration. The book suggests solutions to the difficulties faced by both the Japanese Managers and their European employees and tries to inspire a better working environment for both.

Unlike other books that just describe official Japanese business practices, it tells real stories from real situations, and the consequences of them.

He explains how 14 years as a partner in Formula 1 Motor Racing changed the company and how withdrawal from Formula 1 became an even bigger challenge.

A focus on the handling of personnel and how it differs for Japanese employees and non Japanese employees underlines why foreign companies will always be foreign.

www.ingramcontent.com/pod-product-compliance
Lightning Source LLC
Chambersburg PA
CBHW021620270326
41931CB00008B/796